DELIVERANCE & PRAYER
HANDBOOK FOR CHILDREN
VOL. 1

Securing Children's Destiny
Through
Prayers & Actions

OJ. KUYE

DELIVERANCE & PRAYER
HANDBOOK FOR CHILDREN
VOL. 1

First Written, 2015

ISBN-13: 978-1515197614

Printed in USA

All scriptures in this book are from
New King James Version of the Bible, unless otherwise indicated.

A Publication of
Philson Inc.
The Teaching Ministry of Pastor OJ Kuye
4437 Matthew Road, Grand Prairie, TX 75052 USA
Tel: 1-817-939-1075 | E-mail: ojkuye@aol.com

Cover Design & Book layout by:
Cornerstone Concept and Design, Houston TX
Phone: +1(631)-894-4584 . cornerstoneline@gmail.com
www.thecornerstonepublishers.com

DEDICATION

"But there is a spirit in man and
the inspiration (breath) of the
Almighty gives him understanding."
Job 32:8

This book is dedicated to the Most High God whose spirit upon me inspired and gave understanding to write this book and to all godly parents in past and present generations who have stood firmly in securing the destiny of their children against every form of assault and corruption.

ACKNOWLEDGEMENTS

I deeply acknowledge the immense contributions, by way of support and encouragement, of all significant people in my life, who made the publication of this book a reality. These are my immediate family, friends, colleagues, brethren and loved ones who have in no small measures, made it possible to put this hand book on children's deliverance and prayers in your hand. I pray that the Almighty God sends destiny helpers into their lives and those of their children, in Jesus name.

God Bless!

OJ Kuye
June 2015

CONTENTS

PREFACE

One of the greatest assets of any generation is children. Whatever is precious in life must be protected; otherwise it shall be lost, stolen or destroyed. The destiny of every child is very precious and therefore must be protected from abuse, manipulation, distortion or destruction. In life, there is hardly any success by default. Every story of success is a testament of deliberate action; same with the destiny of children. Children hardly succeed by default or inertia or inaction. Every child who grew up to be successful adult is a product of some deliberate sacrifice of some parent or guardian. Children are indeed the most precious physical gift from God; therefore, their destiny must be protected at all cost and by all means.

Children are so vitally important to God and crucially important to humanity in every generation. God says children are His heritage. In Webster Dictionary of English language, a child is described as a young person especially between infancy and youth. For the purpose of this book, I include as children every individual that has a living parent regardless of the age. If any generation will perpetuate itself in greatness, deliberate attention must be given to the spiritual development and preservation of the destiny of their children. Any family, society or nation that fails to watch out for the destiny of its children has already determined its future for better or for worse.

Failure to nurture children is a success at mortgaging the future of the nation. Because of the vital significance of children in every generation, their destiny must be protected through appropriate moral, social, religious and educational upbringing and appropriate parental action and prayers. There are several books as there are authors on different aspects of child development from a physiological, social, psychological, intellectual and anatomical stand point but few on the spiritual development of children. If we all believe that the spiritual truly controls the physical, then we must not make fasting, praying and taking other appropriate actions for the destiny of our children an afterthought. We must be deliberate about it. We must also combine actions and prayers to achieve the desired result. As it is said, action without prayer is arrogance and prayer without action is hypocrisy. We must pray, watch and take action.

This hand book is divided into two volumes for ease of usage and reference. Volume one examines common issues and appropriate prayers for children from the womb to young adulthood, while volume two examines specific issues and appropriate prayers in adulthood. I pray for total deliverance, safety, protection, provision and progress for our children as we utilize the principles in these books in Jesus name, Amen.

INTRODUCTION

BEST ROLE MODEL AND STRONGEST INFLUENCE

God did not make us fathers and mothers just so the world will not call us barren but God made us parents so we can satisfy a need in His heart for godly seed. We must be the examples of godliness, moral rectitude, uprightness and integrity to our children. We must be their role model. We must lead, teach, instruct and guide them by our example. Mothers should be the best examples and models of godly wives to their daughters, and fathers should be the best examples and models of godly husbands to their sons. Also, we must model responsible living and faithful commitment to relationship to God and others for them, through our actions and prayers. It's said that we can teach what we know but we can only reproduce who we are. Above all, we must not only dedicate our children to the Lord but constantly, frequently and consistently pray for them. I am fortunate to have a mother like Jochebed (Moses' mother) and Susannah Wesley (John Wesley's mother) who took the physical and spiritual upbringing of their children as a ministry, having lost my father when I was about two months old. God preserved my destiny in the face of every kind of physical and spiritual assault, through the actions and prayers of my mother. This is one of my strongest motivation for writing this handbook.

ONCE THE EXAM TAKES PLACE ON A WEDNESDAY, I MUST PASS!

I heard a story from a friend that ministered profoundly to me on this important subject: Some students were preparing for a very important examination in a school. A boy of 4 siblings studied for a while and decided he was going to bed while his class mates were still studying far into the night. His classmates with whom he was studying were surprised at his decision to go to bed. But he told them as long as the teacher put the exam on Wednesday, he would pass and pass very well. 'WHY Wednesday', was the question from his friends. His reply was: 'Mother prays for my siblings and I every day of the week. She dedicates one day for each child and Wednesday is my day when mother prays for me and as long as the examination is on a Wednesday, when its my turn for Mama's prayers, I know I would pass". In deed he wrote the examination on Wednesday and passed very well! This story underscores the significance of parental prayer in the destiny of children.

PARENTING THROUGH LIFE

Speaking about the ever present but dynamic role of parents over their children, Phyllis Diller said: "we spend the first 12 months of our children's lives teaching them to walk and talk and the next 12 months teaching them to sit down and shut up". I believe parenting role never ends, just like the fatherly role of God our father for us as His children never ends. Just like God parental responsibility over children is from the cradle to the grave. Contents may change from time to time but the basic role remains. The psalmist says in Psalm 48:14, "For this God is our God for ever and ever: he will be our guide even unto death." For this reason, parental responsibility for prayer for the children is for as long as they are alive and they are as well.

MOTHER PRAYING, OJ SNORING AWAY!

I remember when I was much younger and few years in marriage. My mother came visiting us in the city where we lived. The guest room was next to our bedroom and very early in the morning, Mama would wake up and start praying. She would pray for such a long period and to me she wasn't really praying. I used to think, 'how could someone be praying for such a long period?' One day, I was woken up by her prayers and I decided to listen attentively, and I discovered that she was praying for each and everyone of her children separately mentioning their names in prayers, when it was that individual's turn. She then went on to pray for all her loved ones and their family, her church, the Pastor and his family and others. So I saw how and why she could pray for long without repeating herself, she had a long laundry list of prayer points! Meanwhile Mama was praying over me and I was snoring away! Indeed in those days, her prayer was my alarm clock to wake up for work. I later understood and saw the spiritual significance of her prayers in those days especially through all the environmental dangers and career challenges that God miraculously delivered our family from. Indeed, the effectual and fervent prayers of parents avail much. I recommend this spiritual pill for all parents and where you have not yet seen the desired result, add more dosage. It works!

CHILDREN ARE GOD'S HERITAGE, NOT PARENT'S HERITAGE

We must influence our children for the Lord. We must not be over- protective of our children. Allow them some freedom, even freedom to make mistakes. They will learn from them. Guide them. Learn to trust them and also trust God to help them make the right choices. They are God's heritage not father or mother's heritage. You are not going to be around them all their lives, so point their attention towards God so they can learn to live independently by trusting God and not you for their sustenance.

No child is perfect neither are you. Don't report the weakness and faults of your children to everyone and anyone, except those that you believe love them and they respect enough to hold them accountable for their behavior. Be their path-finder and not just fault-finder.

Advise them, counsel them, teach them, correct them, encourage them, reward their good behavior. But do not be over-bearing.

LOSING OUR SLEEP WHILE SHE WAS ENJOYING HERSELF!

I remember when our first daughter went to college.

Just like any other child just tasting freedom away from home. They want to enjoy that freedom to the maximum. For several days, she would not call, her mother was calling, but she would neither pick the call nor return her voice messages. Then Saturday night came and we were already in bed, about to sleep. Then my wife complained strongly. "I can't get to talk to this girl for several days and you want to sleep!" My reply had always been: "I am sure she is fine wherever she is." But she was complaining aloud and would not let me sleep because she herself would not.

She continued to call her phone and behold she picked it up and there were some stadium noises at the background and I was curious. I asked her, ' where are you guys?' Her response was: 'We are here at our football stadium enjoying a great game! OU is playing Texas Tech!' The critical lesson and profound truth came home to us that day: Children are God's heritage, not ours. He knows how to protect his heritage once we have done our job well at the early stages of their lives; we don't need to put ourselves in bondage of fear for their well being. At that stage, we are only to pray, committing them to God's hand and advise them where we see the need.

YOU CAN PRESERVE THE DESTINY OF YOUR CHILDREN FROM ASSAULT

I strongly believe from observation and experience that the destiny of children can be preserved from every form of physical and spiritual assault through deliberate actions like training, fasting and prayers. We have seen wonderful destiny spring forth through prayers over children and we have also seen children's destiny bastardized for lack or neglect of spiritual attention through discipline and prayers of parents. For this reason, training, fasting and praying for our children must be a habit.

Many great adults today are products of parental sacrifice in prayers. Many parents travail in prayers for their children from the womb, and the testimony of those prayers are the responsible adults of today. Praying for our children is a responsibility that God has given every godly parent, and there is enormous benefit from discharging this huge responsibility.

Most successful parents also combine prayers with action in raising successful children and successful adults. Moses' mother combined the two. Moses' mother built an ark for the protection of Moses her son, when other Hebrew infant sons were being killed at birth. She took a grave risk that preserved the destiny of Moses (Exodus 2:1-11). The children of Rechab were instructed by their father, Jonadab, and they listened so much that when they found themselves in a foreign land, under no parental supervision, they adhered strictly to the instructions of their parents, and God recorded their obedience for posterity, and it was well with them (Jeremiah 35:3-10)

SOME PARENTS WHO TOOK APPROPRIATE ACTIONS REGARDING THE DESTINY OF THEIR CHILDREN.

- Abraham in the life of Isaac
- Isaac in the life of his children
- Jacob in the life of all his children and grand children
- Jochebed, the mother of Moses
- Esther and her uncle and guardian, Mordecai.
- The Rechabites children and their parents
- Hannah in the life of Samuel
- David in the life of Solomon
- Joseph and Mary in the life of Jesus
- The Mark Chapter 9 father and his dead child and Jesus' intervention
- Timothy and his mother: Eunice, and grandmother: Lois

SOME PARENTS WHO TOOK WRONG ACTION OR FAILED TO TAKE ANY ACTION

- Prophet Eli regarding his children
- Samuel regarding his children
- Manoah regarding his son, Samson
- The father of the prodigal child

We shall be referring to these and other examples as we go through this prayer manual to serve as a reference of godly parenting and otherwise.

GENERAL AND SPECIFIC PRAYERS

Prayers for children from biblical reference were by way of thanksgiving, intercession, petition, prophetic declaration and words of blessings spoken over their destiny.

For example, the patriarch Abraham prayed for the covenant child Isaac to be born, he also indirectly prayed for a bride for Isaac, by extracting an oath of diligent obedience from his chief servant, Elaazar. Isaac prayed to receive the covenant children in Jacob and Essau. Isaac blessed his son Jacob when he was about to die in Genesis 27: 28-29. It was a covenant prayer. Jacob blessed Joseph's sons, Manasseh and Ephraim. Indeed he laid his hands on them as he pronounced blessing upon their lives in

Genesis 48:12-16. He thereafter called all his twelve sons together and made prophetic declaration over their destinies in Genesis Chapter 49:1-27. Indeed, the life they all lived thereafter conformed to the prophetic declaration of their father. Moses stood in the position of spiritual father to bless each one of the tribes of Israel in Deuteronomy 33:6-29. He also laid hands on Joshua as a prophetic action of blessing in Deuteronomy 34:9. So we see the examples in the Patriarchs blessing their biological and spiritual children in the Bible. This reminds me of an experience my father in the Lord, Pastor E. A. Adeboye, always share with us as a reminder of the significance of the prayers of mothers over their children. According to him, while growing up, he says he remembers the mother's prayer for him that when he calls on one person, thousands will answer to him. This was a prayer by way of a prophetic declaration over his destiny. His destiny eventually responded to that declaration. If he calls on one person today, I believe, to be modest, hundreds of thousands will respond to him if not millions!

The bible records some prayers of parents especially the patriarchs over their children, while the bible also records for posterity, those who failed to do so and the consequence of their inaction or neglect. It's said that God will not do anything on this side of eternity except in response to the prayers of men. Prayer is recommended daily, weekly, monthly and yearly for the safety, protection, preservation and success of children, and parents should be the first responder to this responsibility.

This book is essentially a handbook of prayer for children and it is recommended for every parent who desires to see their God-given heritage mature into responsible and successful adult. My prayer is that as we use this book, the destinies of our children shall find expression in the prayers and prophetic declaration, in Jesus name.

CHAPTER 1

FOUNDATION: REINFORCING GODLY FOUNDATION AND UPROOTING EVIL INHERITANCE

We may not be able to prepare the future for our children, but we can at least prepare our children for the future.

- US President Franklin D. Roosevelt

Every human being has a foundation, and every successful journey starts with a good foundation, much so for the journey of life and destiny. It's said that you cannot put up a bigger or taller structure than the foundation laid for it because depth determines height. For this reason, the success of every child depends on the foundation we give him or her. Strong foundation for children is the sole responsibility of parents. This foundation starts with ensuring that two believers, with godly foundation get married to each other. That was one of the saving graces of Moses destiny. The father, Imram and mother, Jochebed had strong spiritual pedigree. Both father and mother were from the priesthood lineage of Levi. Children of God must not be unequally yoked with unbelievers because the foundation will affect their future and that of their children. It's said that if you have an unbeliever for a spouse, you already chose the devil for an in law and you cannot prevent that in law from coming to your home or live with you.

SCRIPTURES FOR MEDITATION

1 Corinthians 3:10-11 KJV

[10] According to the grace of God which is given unto me, as a wise masterbuilder, I have laid the foundation, and another buildeth thereon. But let every man take heed how he buildeth thereupon. [11] For other foundation can no man lay than that is laid, which is Jesus Christ.

I Timothy 6:19 NKJV

Storing up for themselves a good foundation for the time to come, that they may lay hold on eternal life.

Psalms 11:3 NKJV

If the foundations are destroyed, What can the righteous do?

Proverbs 20:7 NKJV

The righteous man walks in his integrity; His children are blessed after him.

Psalms 103:17 NKJV

But the mercy of the LORD is from everlasting to everlasting On those who fear Him, And His righteousness to children's children,

Exodus 20:5-6 NKJV

You shall not bow down to them (idols) nor serve them. For I, the LORD your God, am a jealous God, visiting the iniquity of the fathers upon the children to the third and fourth generations of those who hate Me, but showing mercy to thousands, to those who love Me and keep My commandments.

Exodus 34:6-7 NKJV

And the LORD passed before him and proclaimed, "The LORD, the LORD God, merciful and gracious, longsuffering, and abounding in goodness and truth, keeping mercy for thousands, forgiving iniquity and transgression and sin, by no means clearing the guilty, visiting the iniquity of the fathers upon the children and the children's children to the third and the fourth generation."

Psalms 22:30 NKJV

A seed shall serve Him. It will be recounted of the Lord to the next generation

Matthew 7:24-27 NKJV

"Therefore whoever hears these sayings of Mine, and does them, I will liken him to a wise man who built his house on the rock: and the rain descended, the floods came, and the winds blew and beat on that house; and it did not fall, for it was founded on the rock. "But everyone who hears these sayings of Mine, and does not do them, will be like a foolish man who built his house on the sand: and the rain descended, the floods came, and the winds blew and beat on that house; and it fell. And great was its fall."

Job 5:3-4,7 KJV

I have seen the foolish taking root: but suddenly I cursed his habitation. His children are far from safety, and they are crushed in the gate, neither is there any to deliver them . Yet man is born unto trouble, as the sparks fly upward.

Ezekiel 18:1-4 KJV

The word of the Lord came unto me again, saying, What mean ye, that ye use this proverb concerning the land of Israel, saying, The fathers have eaten sour grapes, and the children's teeth are set on edge? As I live, saith the Lord God , ye shall not have occasion any more to use this proverb in Israel. Behold, all souls are mine; as the soul of the father, so also the soul of the son is mine: the soul that sinneth, it shall die.

Lamentations 5:7-9 KJV

Our fathers have sinned, and are not; and we have borne their iniquities. Servants have ruled over us: there is none that doth deliver us out of their hand. We gat our bread with the peril of our lives because of the sword of the wilderness.

Matthew 15:13 NKJV

But He answered and said, "Every plant which My heavenly Father has not planted will be uprooted.

MAX JUKES & JONATHAN EDWARD DESCENDANTS IN COMPARISON

Max Jukes

"Max Jukes an atheist, lived a godless life in the 1700. He married an ungodly girl. From that union, the following generational offspring were produced in the lineage:

- 7 murderers

- 60 thieves
- 50 women prostitutes
- 130 convicted criminals
- 310 paupers (who spent an aggregate of over 2,300 years in poor houses)
- 400 who were physically wrecked by indulgent living, drunkenness etc.
- His 540 known descendants cost the United States government $1,250,000"

Jonathan Edward

"Jonathan Edward (a leading revivalist) and his wife Sarah, a godly woman, lived at the same time in the 1700 with atheist Max Jukes. An investigation of his 1,394 known descendants from their 11 children produced the following:

- 1 Vice President of the United States of America
- 3 United States Senators
- 3 State Governors
- 3 Mayors
- 13 College Presidents
- 65 College Professors
- 30 Judges
- 100 Lawyers
- 60 Medical Doctors
- 75 Navy Officers
- 100 Preachers and Missionaries

- 60 Authors of prominence
- 80 Public Officers in other capacities
- 295 University graduates among whom were United States Representatives to foreign countries, etc. None of his descendants cost the United States government a cent".

(Information from "Jukes-Edwards: A Study in Education and Heredity" written by A.E. Winship in 1900 and also used in the sermon "Leadership Defined" in the series Leadership: The Surprising Influence of a Godly Life).

This study clearly shows the profound effect of a godly foundation on generational legacy. Every parent must make a commitment to godly life and lifestyle. That is the first assurance for a godly offspring.

Billy Graham: 10 A.m. Prayer Rituals by Father & Mother!

Billy Graham is the legendary Evangelist of our generation. He is reputed to have been used by God to lead over 3 million people to Christ, and preached the gospel to more than 80 million people in his lifetime! According to him, his mother, Morrow Graham had the greatest influence on his life. "She would gather the family to listen to the bible and have prayers together in the presence of God." She and his father would pray for Billy at 10 o'clock every morning.

An African adage says, 'if someone sows a seed of wickedness, his children will eat of the harvest'. I believe the same goes for seed of goodness. For this reason, parents must be careful about their seed.

While individuals can enjoy the benefit of their godly ways, they can also benefit from the godliness of their parents, grandparents and great grandparents. In the same manner, individuals bear the consequences of their sins, but they also suffer for the sins, wickedness or idolatry of their parents, grandparents, great grandparents, and the same God ensures and supervises the enforcement of the two different consequences. Some people have suffered hardship in life because of the wicked ways of their ancestors, until they knew the truth and got delivered from such generational yoke of affliction. For this reason, every parent must ensure that they build a godly and righteous foundation for themselves and the generations coming after them.

In **Genesis 12:1**, God told Abraham to get out of his father's house before he could be blessed. His father's house was a house of idolatry. In **Judges 6:25-32**, God told Gideon to burn down the idol of his father's house and to build an alter to Jehovah God before his destiny and that of the nation could be rehabilitated.

For this reason, parent must deliberately ensure their right standing with God through our Lord Jesus Christ and also do a critical self examination of their spiritual foundation to correct any wrong that may be traceable to idolatry, ungodliness, unrighteousness or wickedness through corrective personal action and spiritual exercise.

PRAYER POINTS

1. Father, thank you for the gift of life and for preserving my spirit, soul and body to witness today amongst the living.
2. Father, thank you for the parents and the lineage through which you have brought me into the world
3. Father, thank you for the life of every one in my lineage, both in present and past generations. Thank you for those you have saved and those we are believing you to save their lives.
4. Lord Jesus, I confess and repent of my sins, have mercy on me, in Jesus' name.
5. Lord Jesus, I confess of the sins of my father and mother, have mercy on them, in Jesus' name.

6. Lord Jesus, I identify with the sins of my ancestors and lineage, I repent on their behalf and I pray for your mercy in Jesus' name.
7. Lord Jesus, by your blood, wash me, wash my father, wash my mother, wash my family and forgive the sins of my ancestors; their wickedness, evil ways and all forms of transgressions, in Jesus' name.
8. Father, cleanse my family line of every form of idolatry and wickedness by the precious blood of your only begotten son, Jesus Christ.
9. Father, sanitize my ancestral line and lineage of every form of ungodliness and evil records, in Jesus name.
10. I release myself and my children from every inherited and generational bondage, in the name of Jesus.
11. In the name of Jesus, I command you idol of my father's house and mother's house to lose your hold over my life and over the life of my children.
12. Every 'strong man' of my father's and mother's house, die now, in the name of Jesus.
13. I severe every linkage to ancestral evil altar, evil worship, evil sacrifice and idolatrous worship of my mother's house and father's house, in Jesus name.
14. Every evil handwriting and satanic ordinances

of my father's house and mother's house, be wiped away now, in the name of Jesus.

15. Every evil covenant of my father's house and mother's house working against my progress and those of my children is hereby revoked, in the name of Jesus.
16. Father, send your heavenly carpenter to the foundation of my life to dismantle every ancestral evil establishment, in Jesus name.
17. I command the blood of Jesus to flush out from my system and those of my children every inherited evil deposit and satanic build up, in Jesus name.
18. I break every inherited curse of my father's and mother's house operating over my life and those of my children, in the name of Jesus.
19. It is written that the rod of the wicked shall not rest upon the lot of the righteous. Therefore, no rod of the wicked ones from my father's house or mother's house shall rest upon me or my children, in Jesus name.
20. I decree against every generational carryover of the satanic effect of 'sour grape' eating syndrome by my father or mother. Your effect is hereby and herewith terminated, in Jesus' name.
21. My children shall not suffer from 'sour grape' syndrome, their teeth shall not be set on edge,

in Jesus name.

22. I silence the voice of foundational strong men of my father's house and mother's house. It shall not affect my children, in Jesus' name.
23. I decree total paralyses of activities of satanic stronghold set against me or my children, in Jesus name.
24. I release my children from every evil disposition and evil domination of my father's house and mother's house, in Jesus name.
25. By way of prophetic action, I burn down every altar of evil of my father's house and mother's house. They shall never work against my children, in Jesus name.
26. By the power of the Holy Ghost, I severe my destiny and that of my children from evil dedication, parental curses, inherited infirmity, demonic exchange of destiny, demonic marriage, generational family animosity, siblings rivalry, satanic corruption of genes, strange behavior, evil addiction, strange appetite, sexual perversion, destructive consequence of polygamy and common lineage spiritual problems, barrenness, inherited anger, delay, evil initiation and demonic dedication, in Jesus name.
27. In Jesus' name, I shut now, every satanic door granting access to evil occurrences against me

or my children.

28. Every strange and ancestral god's and idols of my father's and mother's house causing evil manifestation in my life and those of my children, your time is up. Scatter by fire now, in the name of Jesus,
29. I uproot now every tree which is not the planting of the Lord in my foundation, from my father's or mother's house, in the name of Jesus.
30. I terminate by the fire of the Holy Ghost, every fruit such evil tree could have produced in my lineage in the name of Jesus.
31. I open the door of deliverance, healing, progress, promotion and advancement, success and significance in every sphere of life for my children, in Jesus name.
32. Father, I thank you for answered prayers and for your mighty deliverance of my children from generational yoke and foundational bondage, in Jesus name.

CHAPTER 2

CHOICE OF LIFE PARTNER: PRAYING FOR GODLY SPOUSE

We never know the love of the parent till we become parents ourselves.

- Henry Ward Beecher

Godly children are products of godly individuals who come together to produce godly union, which in turn produces godly children. The project of producing godly, successful children starts from making a godly choice of spouse. It's the law of nature that every living thing will reproduce after its kind. Good and godly choice of marriage partner has been known to establish and make people's destiny to blossom while bad choices of partners have also been known to sabotage an otherwise beautiful destiny. For this reason, there must be deliberate and concerted prayers regarding the choice of marriage partner, because it's a life-long commitment and relationship.

When it was time for Isaac to get married, his father Abraham sent his chief servant Eliazar to go to the country of his birth to get a wife for Isaac, from among his people. He did, and hence got Rebecca as wife for Isaac. That union produced the the next patriarch in Jacob who became the father of the twelve tribes of Israel. The instruction of God is very clear on marriage. We should not be unequally yoked neither should our children. For this reason, we must deliberately pray and guide our children by the help of God to marry the right person and into the right family.

Jochebed, the mother of Moses married right, Isaac, the father of Jacob married right. The result was very obvious in the children regarding the destiny of their offspring.

SCRIPTURAL FOR MEDITATION

Genesis 24:2-4 KJV

> And Abraham said unto his eldest servant of his house, that ruled over all that he had, Put, I pray thee, thy hand under my thigh: And I will make thee swear by the Lord ,

the God of heaven, and the God of the earth, that thou shalt not take a wife unto my son of the daughters of the Canaanites, among whom I dwell: But thou shalt go unto my country, and to my kindred, and take a wife unto my son Isaac.

Exodus 2:1-2 NKJV

And a man of the house of Levi went and took as wife a daughter of Levi. So the woman conceived and bore a son. And when she saw that he was a beautiful child, she hid him three months.

Joshua 24:15 KJV

And if it seem evil unto you to serve the Lord , choose you this day whom ye will serve; whether the gods which your fathers served that were on the other side of the flood, or the gods of the Amorites, in whose land ye dwell: but as for me and my house, we will serve the Lord.

Psalm 47:4 KJV

He shall choose our inheritance for us, the excellency of Jacob whom he loved.

Psalm 48:14 KJV

For this God is our God for ever and ever: he will be our guide even unto death.

Isaiah 30:21 KJV

And thine ears shall hear a word behind

thee, saying, This is the way, walk ye in it, when ye turn to the right hand, and when ye turn to the left.

Psalm 16:7 KJV

I will bless the Lord , who hath given me counsel: my reins also instruct me in the night seasons.

Psalm 32:8 KJV

I will instruct thee and teach thee in the way which thou shalt go: I will guide thee with mine eye.

2 Corinthians 6:14 KJV

Be ye not unequally yoked together with unbelievers: for what fellowship hath righteousness with unrighteousness? and what communion hath light with darkness?

The union of two descendants of the house of Levi, family of priests produced Moses, whom God would later use to deliver His people from several years of collective and institutional captivity and bondage, in the hands of Pharaoh.

AFFLICTION OF GRANDFATHER'S HOUSE CAME UPON DESCENDANTS

Growing up, I discovered that women in my extended family did not marry right. Most women married lazy or irresponsible men. Yet most men in my extended family lived responsibly especially when it came to marital relationships and obligations. When I came to know the Lord better, this became a big burden to me, and I deliberately began to seek the face of God regarding why this noticeable pattern was so. God later opened my eyes to some truths around my paternal grandfather's house.

Grandfather had several male children, and all the children of my father's generation got married and brought their wives to our family's big compound to live. I later discovered that all the women married into grandfather's house just like all Africans in that generation had their root in idolatry. Thank God grandfather came to know the Lord and was at a time the grand patron of one of the local church in our community, but most women in our homes brought their strange ancestral gods to grandfather's house. I grew up still seeing them making sacrifices to those gods. There was Sango, Oro, Ogun, Ifa etc. Most brought their family idols into grandfather's house ignorantly and some deliberately.

The Lord inspired me to confront this issue in prayers and fasting to break and destroy the negative consequences of those idolatrous background issues and any evil manifestation on subsequent generations. God honored my sacrifice of obedience to His instructions and answered my prayers. He set our family tree free from the evil effects of foundation of idolatry, which consequence affected the marital destiny of our female children. The yoke was broken to the glory of God. It is not only important to marry the right person, but also important to marry into the right family.

PRAYER POINTS

1. Thank God for preserving your life to see your children attain the age of marriage.
2. Thank God for preserving the life of your children to see the age of marriage.
3. Confess common marital sins of your fathers like lust, adultery, incest and all kinds of marital perversion.
4. Lord, it is written in your word, you will be my guide from now even unto the end, we receive divine guidance regarding marriage partners for my children, in the name of Jesus
5. Father, instruct and guide my children regarding the choice of marriage partner, in the name of Jesus.
6. Father, let your reins, let your Spirit, instruct my children regarding the choice of life partners,

in Jesus' name.

7. Lord, divinely align the steps of my child to the godly life partner you have divinely ordained for him/her, in the name of Jesus.
8. Father, cause my children to be patient for you as you instruct them concerning their choices of life partners, in the name of Jesus.
9. Father, I pray for godly patience to come upon my son (Name......) / my daughter (Name....) until the godly ordained partner shows up, in the name of Jesus.
10. Father, I rebuke every spirit of hurriedness, impatience over my children as regards marital choices, in the name of Jesus.
11. Lord, break every satanic blockage, barricade and barrier keeping my children from meeting, seeing and recognizing their godly ordained partners. Let every such satanic barrier be shattered now, in the name of Jesus.
12. Father, you have made and assigned the right persons for my children to marry, let such individuals come forth, without delay, in the name of Jesus.
13. Father, let that divine match you have preordained for my son/daughter manifest now, in the name of Jesus.
14. I stand in the gap and call forth my son/ daughter into his/her marital destiny now, in

the name of Jesus.

15. I stand in the gap and call out your ordained partner for my son/daughter from hiding or obscurity now, in the name of Jesus.
16. Father, I reject for my son/my daughter, counterfeit spouse, fake spouse, deceiving spouse, hypocrite spouse, chameleonic spouse, ungodly spouse, in the name of Jesus.
17. Father I pray for the spirit of discernment upon my son (Name...) and my daughter (Name...) to be divinely guided in his/her choice, in the name of Jesus.
18. Lord, command the forces of heaven to destroy every ancestral linkage to evil choices of partners, in the name of Jesus.
19. Father, I decree prophetically a godly spouse for my son (Name.....) and my daughter (Name.....), in the name of Jesus.
20. Father, I decree prophetically a God fearing spouse for my son (Name.....) and my daughter (Name.....), in the name of Jesus.
21. Father, I decree prophetically a responsible spouse for my son (Name.....) and my daughter (Name.....), in the name of Jesus.
22. Father, I decree prophetically a visionary spouse for my son (Name.....) and my daughter (Name.....), in the name of Jesus.
23. I decree an end to any relationship or association

or friendship with the wrong person as regards marital intention for my son/daughter now, in the name of Jesus.

24. Father, you helped the destiny of Moses by supernaturally enabling two individuals of the house of Levi to meet, help the destiny and future of my children by supernaturally enabling them to be joined in marital relationship to godly partners, in the name of Jesus.
25. Father, you helped Abraham and Sarah get a good spouse in Rebecca for their son Isaac, help us O God in getting a good spouse for our son/daughter, in the name of Jesus.
26. By your divine help, Isaac married a godly spouse from the right families, cause our children to marry godly spouses and from the right families, in Jesus name.
27. By the power of the most high God, I come against every form of unprofitable delay and lateness in my children getting married, in the name of Jesus.
28. In the name of Jesus, I break every evil linkage to spiritual husband or spiritual wife exercising authority over my life or my children's life, in the name of Jesus.
29. I am the excellence of Jacob that you loved, thank you for choosing my marital inheritance

for me, in the name of Jesus.

30. Father, thank you for securing the marital destiny of our son (Name....) and our daughter (Name.......) by bringing the right person from the right family into marital relationship with them.
31. Father, thank you for all answered prayers, in the mighty of Jesus.

CHAPTER 3

FRUITFULNESS: PRAYING FOR TIMELY CONCEPTION AND GODLY CHILDREN

The value of marriage is not that adults produce children, but that children produce adults.

- Peter De Vries

The desire of God for couples in marriages according to **Malachi 2:15 NKJV**, is to bring forth godly children. From this scriptural stand point, one can desire and pray for conception and bringing forth of covenant children. Hannah did and God granted her desire.

I have seen from experience that God is consistently committed to fulfilling the God-pleasing desire of His children, including the fruit of the womb. I desired that God will bless me with a daughter for our first child when I got married, and God was kind and gracious to grant my heart desire by blessing us with a baby girl. We had desired to have two children. So God in fulfilling our desire blessed my wife with her second pregnancy. She asked me, "what sex do you desire? boy or girl?" I said the sex did not bother me as long as God gave us a healthy baby. It pleased God to bless us with a healthy baby girl for our second child, and we thanked God and thought that we had finished with that business. But God had some other plans.

GOD MAY GIVE YOU WHAT YOU DON'T PRAY FOR IF HE KNOWS THAT WILL MAKE YOUR LIFE COMPLETE

About seven years after the birth of our second child, we thought we had put appropriate 'safeguard' for my wife not to become pregnant, but God by His sovereign will broke through our 'safeguard and barricade'. My wife became pregnant with our third child when we were at our mid ages. The pregnancy came with the natural tendencies of mid age pregnancy crisis but God prevailed for us such that she was able to carry the pregnancy through and behold it was a baby boy, given by the Lord Himself, and that is why we refer to our three children as covenant children. They were all products of God's faithfulness. My prayer is that any blessing you may not pray or ask for but which God knows will make your life complete will be ushered into your life in this season, in Jesus name.

In many cases, we have seen several people pray to God for the blessing of children. The patriarch Abraham had a dialogue with God regarding the everlasting covenant of generational blessing and the barren state of Sarah, and God supernaturally visited the wife and blessed Sarah with the miraculous, nature-defying pregnancy of Isaac **(Genesis 15:1-6, 221:1-7)**. Isaac interceded for Rebekah, the wife, who was barren and the result of the prayers was the miraculous birth of the twins, Esau and Jacob **(Genesis 25:21).** Hannah, who was also barren, prayed in Shiloh and also made a vow to the Lord for the miracle of Samuel. God heard her prayers and honored her sacrifice of vow by blessing her with the pregnancy which produced Samuel, the great prophet **(1 Samuel 1:1-20).** There are countless examples around us today of miraculous conception and delivery of miracle children after several years of barrenness. As many of us are believing God and praying for the first child or more children, the Almighty God will hearken unto our voice like Isaac and Hannah and bless us with our pregnancies, in Jesus mighty name.

All these people not only prayed but they coupled their prayers with action. As it is said, prayer without action is hypocrisy and action without prayer is arrogance.

We must be ready to pray and take appropriate God-inspired actions for our expected fruit of the womb, which is a heritage of the Lord.

SCRIPTURE FOR MEDITATION

Genesis 1:28 NKJV

Then God blessed them, and God said to them, "Be fruitful and multiply; fill the earth and subdue it; have dominion over the fish of the sea, over the birds of the air, and over every living thing that moves on the earth."

Genesis 21:1-3, 6NKJV

And the LORD visited Sarah as He had said, and the LORD did for Sarah as He had spoken. For Sarah conceived and bore Abraham a son in his old age, at the set time of which God had spoken to him. And Abraham called the name of his son who was born to him—whom Sarah bore to him— Isaac.

And Sarah said, "God has made me laugh, and all who hear will laugh with me."

Genesis 25:21 NKJV

Now Isaac pleaded with the LORD for his wife, because she was barren; and the LORD granted his plea, and Rebekah his wife conceived.

Exodus 23:25-26 NKJV

"So you shall serve the LORD your God, and He will bless your bread and your water. And I will take sickness away from the midst of you. No one shall suffer miscarriage or be barren in your land; I will fulfill the number of your days.

Deuteronomy 7:14 NKJV

You shall be blessed above all peoples; there shall not be a male or female barren among you or among your livestock.

Judges 13:3 NKJV

And the Angel of the LORD appeared to the woman and said to her, "Indeed now, you are barren and have borne no children, but you shall conceive and bear a son.

I Samuel 1:19-20 NKJV

Then they rose early in the morning and worshiped before the LORD, and returned and came to their house at Ramah. And Elkanah knew Hannah his wife, and the

LORD remembered her. So it came to pass in the process of time that Hannah conceived and bore a son, and called his name Samuel, saying, "Because I have asked for him from the LORD."

1 Samuel 2:5 NKJV

Those who were full have hired themselves out for bread, And the hungry have ceased to hunger. Even the barren has borne seven, And she who has many children has become feeble.

Psalms 30:5 NKJV

For His anger is but for a moment, His favor is for life; Weeping may endure for a night, But joy comes in the morning.

Psalms 113:9 NKJV

He grants the barren woman a home, Like a joyful mother of children. Praise the LORD!

Isaiah 32:15 NKJV

Until the Spirit is poured upon us from on high, And the wilderness becomes a fruitful field, And the fruitful field is counted as a forest.

Malachi 2:15 NKJV

But did He not make them one, Having a remnant of the Spirit? And why one? He seeks godly offspring. Therefore take heed to your spirit, And let none deal treacherously with the wife of his youth.

Luke 1:36-37 NKJV

Now indeed, Elizabeth your relative has also conceived a son in her old age; and this is now the sixth month for her who was called barren. For with God nothing will be impossible."

Psalms 90:14 NKJV

Oh, satisfy us early with Your mercy, That we may rejoice and be glad all our days!

PRAYER POINTS

1. Offer thanksgiving prayers to the Lord for the opportunity of seeing your children getting married to the bone of their bone and the flesh of their flesh
2. Offer thanksgiving prayers for successful marriage ceremonies for your child
3. Offer thanksgiving prayers for the godly home and environment of love and unity God is creating for them in marriage.
4. Father, I thank you for entrusting these children to me as biological parent.
5. Father, I confess on behalf of my children of their past sins arising from bad choices, which could affect their marital destiny, in the name of Jesus.

6. Father, by your mercy, deliver my children from harvesting the seed of their past sins and iniquity, in the name of Jesus.
7. As spiritual seed of Abraham, I decree that my children shall be fruitful and multiply, in the name of Jesus.
8. Father, I and my children are under a divine mandate to be fruitful and multiply, and we shall be fruitful and multiply, in the name of Jesus.
9. Father, I decree against the spirit of delay to conception and pregnancy concerning my children, in the name of Jesus.
10. Father, on the authority of your word, none of my children shall be barren, in Jesus name.
11. I decree immediate conception after consummation of marriage, in the name of Jesus.
12. Father, out of the loins of my son shall come forth godly children in accordance with your word, in the name of Jesus.
13. Father, out of the womb of my daughter shall bring forth godly children in accordance with your word, in Jesus' name.
14. Father, I decree into the reproductive organs of my daughter (Name....) to bring forth immediately, in the name of Jesus.

15. Father, in your name, I decree to the Fallopian tube, the womb, the uterus of my daughters to become fertile, in the name of Jesus.
16. O God, guide my children through the child-bearing process, in the name of Jesus.
17. Every generational yoke of delayed fruitfulness and child-bearing is destroyed now, in the name of Jesus.
18. Father, frustrate and destroy every plan and every action of the evil one to stop me or my daughter from conceiving, in the name of Jesus.
19. Father, let every evil pattern of barrenness in my linage die now, in the name of Jesus.
20. In the name of Jesus, I decree a supernatural touch upon my womb/ my child's womb, against every spirit that turns the womb to a cemetery, in the name of Jesus.
21. Father, I decree a supernatural touch upon my loins; let every low sperm count be converted to full sperm count and correct every genealogical abnormality in my reproductive organs now, in the name of Jesus.
22. My womb/my child's womb is meant to carry babies, and that shall be so in the name of Jesus.
23. I decree upon my womb/my child's womb, you shall incubate and carry normal, healthy and perfect child, in the name of Jesus.

24. Father, I decree against every form of abnormal growth in my reproductive/my child's reproductive organs, in the name of Jesus.
25. I decree that my womb/my daughter's womb, uterus and breast begin to function according to divine mandate, in the name of Jesus.
26. The Angel of the Lord visited Sarah and she conceived and brought forth miraculously in spite of natural barrier; father send my angel of destiny now, in the name of Jesus.
27. Father, when you visited Sarah, you gave her laughter, as you visit me/my daughter this month, this season, this year, turn my sorrow/ my children's sorrow to joy and my mourning/ my children's mourning to laughter, in the name of Jesus.
28. God visited Hannah after several years of barrenness, and she conceived and brought forth the miracle of Samuel; father, visit me/my children and remove every yoke of bareness, in the name of Jesus.
29. Hannah prayed the right prayer that changed her destiny forever; father inspire me/my children to pray the right prayer to turn around every form of bareness in my life/my children's lives, in the name of Jesus.
30. Father, thank you for making me/my daughter

to fulfill the divine mandate for fruitfulness.

31. Father, thank you that you have made me/my children fruitful and thank you because the curse of delay has been broken, in Jesus name.

CHAPTER 4

PREGNANCY & CHILDBIRTH: PRAYING FOR SAFE & HEALTHY DELIVERY

There are only two lasting bequeaths we can hope to give to our children, one of these is root, the other wings.

- Author Unknown

It is not enough to pray for miraculous conception to bring an end to barrenness, one must pray more importantly to bring forth healthy children in safe and sound condition. This also includes prayer to live and witness the celebration of the joy. We have seen occasions where the living has been taking out of the dead or the dead out of the living, by the operation of satanic interception and evil visitation during the maturation or gestation period, or at the point of delivery. There are still spiritual Pharaohs manifesting in different styles, to destroy the 'Moses' of their generation. There are still spiritual Herods today waiting to destroy the destiny of little 'Jesus' of this generation.

We have also seen several situations of bringing forth of abnormal, medically or physically challenged babies, or deformed babies due to complications at the point of delivery or due to physiological reasons. There have been all kinds of terrible diagnoses, concerning babies in the womb. For this reason, pregnant women must be sensitive to pray fervently for normal, healthy children and to reject any form of diagnosis that is contrary to divine plans for their babies. Pregnant women must learn to speak life and health and normalcy to their babies in the womb.

There is an African adage that the enemy does not desire a man carrying a heavy load or burden or yoke to put it down; it is one's destiny that helps him set it down. Many suffer miscarriages, some suffer still birth, some give birth but immediately after birth, something terrible will occur and the baby would not live. The joy will immediately be terminated! At times, the mother dies in the process of child birth and joy turns to mourning.

For this reason, there must be pro-activeness in the place of fasting and prayers to carry the pregnancy through and to deliver a healthy baby safely and alive.

The case of Rachel at the birth of Benjamin

In Genesis 35:16-19, we read the tragic account of the death of Rachel in childbirth.

> Then they journeyed from Bethel. And when there was but a little distance to go to Ephrath, Rachel labored in childbirth, and she had hard labor. Now it came to pass, when she was in hard labor, that the midwife said to her, "Do not fear; you will have this son also." And so it was, as her soul was departing (for she died), that she called his name Ben-Oni; but his father called him Benjamin. So Rachel died and was buried on the way to Ephrath (that is, Bethlehem). **Genesis 35:16-19 NKJV**

The Man Born Blind

> And his disciples asked him, saying, Master, who did sin, this man, or his parents, that he was born blind? Jesus answered, Neither hath this man sinned, nor his parents: but that the works of God should be made

manifest in him. **John 9:2-3 KJV**

GOD MIRACULOUSLY DELIVERED AFTER DIAGNOSIS OF ABNORMAL CHILD IN THE WOMB

A close family friend shared their testimony with us about the wonders of our God regarding the birth of their last child. The couple had two boys already, ages 8 and 6 when the wife became pregnant. This couple were servants of God serving faithfully as workers in their local church. The initial test after pregnancy revealed that the child was going to be born challenged with Down syndrome gene disorder. Then the anxiety, crying and emotionally-traumatizing problem started. As the months rolled by, the doctors appealed to the couple to consider aborting the pregnancy but because of their faith, they refused but decided to believe God for a divine intervention.

According to the woman, "as I was confessing the words of God over the baby, I had my secret fears and was weeping in prayers by day and night all through the pregnancy". The trouble was so much upon them that they were less bothered about the sex of the baby, but the challenges they were going to face together to take care of the child through life. On the day of delivery, the Almighty God did that which He alone could do. He supernaturally changed the genotype of the baby in the womb such that the new born baby girl who is now four years old, had no trait of Down syndrome at all! Not even a single genealogical disorder! Now God also granted their heart desire for a baby girl. As the girl was growing up, in school and among her peers, she had always been singled out as the sweetest, smartest and brightest! You can imagine for a child that the doctors put pressure on the parents to abort.

According to the mother, "many who see her growing up as a sweet and very smart child are seeing the glory but did not know the story behind it". How she cried through several days and nights ceaselessly in prayers for God's mercy and intervention. According to her, "I stood on the word of God. Though, I must confess my faith failed at times but God saw my weakness and faithfulness and came through for us. My prayer for someone using this manual is that God will supernaturally intervene, to give you a turn around from every situation that has been giving you concern over any of your children or unborn baby, in the name of Jesus.

SCRIPTURES FOR MEDITATION

Genesis 38:27-30 KJV

And it came to pass in the time of her travail, that, behold, twins were in her womb. And it came to pass, when she travailed, that the one put out his hand: and the midwife took and bound upon his hand a scarlet thread, saying, This came out first. And it came to pass, as he drew back his hand, that, behold, his brother came out: and she said, How hast thou broken forth? this breach be upon thee: therefore his name was called Pharez. And afterward came out his brother, that had the scarlet thread upon his hand: and his name was called Zerah.

Exodus 23:26 NKJV

No one shall suffer miscarriage or be barren in your land; I will fulfill the number of your days.

Psalms 127:3-5 NKJV

Behold, children are a heritage from the LORD, The fruit of the womb is a reward. Like arrows in the hand of a warrior, So are the children of one's youth. Happy is the man who has his quiver full of them; They shall not be ashamed, But shall speak with their enemies in the gate.

Isaiah 65:23 NKJV

They shall not labor in vain, Nor bring forth children for trouble; For they shall be the descendants of the blessed of the LORD, And their offspring with them.

Isaiah 66:7-9 NKJV

"Before she was in labor, she gave birth; Before her pain came, She delivered a male child. Who has heard such a thing? Who has seen such things? Shall the earth be made to give birth in one day? Or shall a nation be born at once? For as soon as Zion was in labor, She gave birth to her children. Shall I bring to the time of birth, and not cause delivery?" says the LORD. "Shall I who cause delivery shut up the womb? " says your God.

Hosea 9:14 NKJV

Give them, O LORD — What will You give? Give them a miscarrying womb And dry breasts!

Luke 1:57-58 NKJV

Now Elizabeth's full time came for her to be delivered, and she brought forth a son. When her neighbors and relatives heard how the Lord had shown great mercy to her, they rejoiced with her.

John 16:21 NKJV

A woman, when she is in labor, has sorrow because her hour has come; but as soon as she has given birth to the child, she no longer remembers the anguish, for joy that a human being has been born into the world.

I Timothy 2:15 NKJV

Nevertheless she will be saved in childbearing if they continue in faith, love, and holiness, with self-control.

Revelation 12:1-2, 4-5

Now a great sign appeared in heaven: a woman clothed with the sun, with the moon under her feet, and on her head a garland of twelve stars. Then being with child, she cried out in labor and in pain to give birth.

His tail drew a third of the stars of heaven and threw them to the earth. And the dragon stood before the woman who was ready to give birth, to devour her Child as soon as it was born. She bore a male Child who was to rule all nations with a rod of iron. And her Child was caught up to God and His throne.

PRAYER POINTS

1. Offer praise and thanksgiving prayers to God for keeping you/your daughter alive to experience the privilege of conception after marriage.
2. Offer praise and thanksgiving prayers to God for making you/your daughter fruitful
3. Offer praise and thanksgiving to God for removing you/your children from the company of the barren
4. Offer praise and thanksgiving prayers to God that His word on fruitfulness and multiplication is finding expression in your life and the lives of your children.
5. Father, by your mercy, wash me/my daughter from every sin and the iniquities of our sins, in the name of Jesus.
6. I decree on the authority of your word, I shall not suffer a miscarriage neither shall my daughter (Name ....)suffer miscarriage of pregnancy, in the name of Jesus.
7. By the fire of the Holy Ghost, I/my daughter and the baby in the womb are shielded from every evil monitoring and progress arrestor, in the name of Jesus.
8. O God, deliver me/my daughter from every pregnancy related sickness: morning sickness,

nauseating, vomiting, dizziness and every form of pregnancy complication, in the name of Jesus.

9. Father, supernaturally correct every abnormality or mal-functioning of my/my children's reproductive organs, in the name of Jesus
10. Father, let every evil pattern of pregnancy failure, miscarriage, still birth, abortion in my linage die now, in the name of Jesus.
11. Father, I decree that no weapon fashioned against my/my daughter's pregnancy shall prosper, in the name of Jesus.
12. Father, I break every stronghold and opposition to my/my daughter's pregnancy, in the name of Jesus.
13. I decree death upon every pregnancy killer or terminator in my life under any guise, in the name of Jesus.
14. I speak prophetically to every organ, tissue, cell, blood vein in me/my daughter to work in harmony and in cooperation throughout this pregnancy and beyond, in the name of Jesus.
15. Every wicked instrument of oppression set to abort my/my daughter's pregnancy, die now, in the name of Jesus.
16. Father, fight every destroyer of fruitfulness and harvest working against my/my daughter's

destiny. Scatter and destroy their operations now, in the name of Jesus.

17. Father, I bind every spirit of miscarriages roaming about my/my daughter's life, in the name of Jesus.
18. Father, on the authority of your word; we shall not cast our young, our young ones in the womb shall not suffer still birth, in the name of Jesus.
19. Father, I decree that I/my daughter shall use our hand to carry living and healthy babies and not to carry dead babies in the name of Jesus.
20. I decree that I/my daughter shall not know the cemetery of our children, in the name of Jesus.
21. I break every hold of witchcraft and the power of the wicked ones over my/my daughter's pregnancy, in the name of Jesus.
22. I decree the peace of the Lord upon my body, throughout pregnancy, I shall not be stressed in the name of Jesus.
23. I come against every form of premature, untimely and abnormal delivery, in the name of Jesus.
24. Elizabeth only brought forth when her time came, my baby shall mature normally and perfectly in the womb, I shall bring forth only when my time comes and not before or after, in the name of Jesus.

25. I come against every form of early contraction or early dilation. Let things happen at nine months due time, in the name of Jesus
26. Father, send your heavenly appointed doctors and nurses and midwives to deliver my/my daughter's baby, in the name of Jesus. I bind every spirit of errors from the hands of doctors and nurses, in the name of Jesus.
27. I decree that out of my womb/my daughter's womb shall come forth normal, healthy and perfect new born baby. I/my daughter shall not bring forth deformed, challenged or abnormal babies, in the name of Jesus,
28. On the authority of your word, I/my daughter shall not labor in vain nor bring forth for trouble. I shall live to nurture my baby. My baby shall not become an orphan from birth, in the name of Jesus.
29. I decree immediate death upon every Pharaoh of my/my daughter's new born baby; perish them in the Red Sea now, in the name of Jesus.
30. I decree immediate extermination of every power of Herod over my/my daughter's new born, in the name of Jesus.
31. Father, let every Herod that seek the life of my/my daughter's new born baby die before the baby is born, in the name of Jesus.
32. Father, completely insulate me/my daughter's

pregnancy from every evil plan and envelope me/my daughter and baby in the womb by your Holy Spirit throughout the pregnancy, in the name of Jesus.

33. Thank you for the great testimony of the birth of a perfect baby and for the joy you have brought into the world through me.
34. Thank you father for answered prayers.

CHAPTER 5

CHRISTENING: PRAYING FOR DESTINY-IMPACTING NAME

A good name is better than precious ointment
- King Solomon

The first and very important step every parent should take is seek the face of God for the name to be given to their new born baby, because of the spiritual significance of names. A child will have to answer to his name from cradle to the grave. Thousands of people will call the name possibly a million times, from birth till the death. Any time a person's name is called and the bearer responds, the destiny responds as well to the meaning of the name. Some bear a particular name in the physical but the spirit realm recognizes them by a different name. As we see from biblical times, children's destiny often conform to the names given to them by their parents. Gideon means warrior, Moses means drawn from the water, Josua means savior or deliverer. We see the destiny of these individuals responding to their given names as they grew up. Its been proven time and again that name does have a direct impact on destiny. That was why God had to change some people's names in the bible while some others changed their names themselves because of the manifestations in adulthood as a direct consequence of their names.

An African adage says you look at the situation prevailing in a family to name a child. I will rather recommend parents look at the future they expect for the child in God to name the child. This is because every situation is subject to change. Choosing a name can be seen as a routine act by parents but we must be serious and deliberate about it. We must seek the face of God and allow God to inspire us by the help of the Holy Spirit for destiny impacting names. Let's take some examples in the bible:
The naming of Abraham, Sarah, Benjamin, Moses, Jacob, Jabez, Nabal and John the Baptist.

ABRAHAM AND SARAH

Genesis 17:5 KJV

Neither shall thy name any more be called Abram, but thy name shall be Abraham; for a father of many nations have I made thee.

Genesis 17:15-16 KJV

And God said unto Abraham, As for Sarai thy wife, thou shalt not call her name Sarai, but Sarah shall her name be . And I will bless her, and give thee a son also of her: yea, I will bless her, and she shall be a mother of nations; kings of people shall be of her.

As long as Abram and Sarai were the names of the patriarch and matriarch respectively, there was bareness in their lives until God appeared to them and changed their names to Abraham and Sarah, meaning father and mother of multitude of nations.

BENJAMIN

Genesis 35:16-19 NKJV

Then they journeyed from Bethel. And when there was but a little distance to go to Ephrath, Rachel labored in childbirth, and she had hard labor. Now it came to pass, when she was in hard labor, that the midwife said to her, "Do not fear; you will have this son also." And so it was, as her soul was departing (for she died), that she called his name Ben-Oni; but his father called him Benjamin. So Rachel died and was buried on the way to Ephrath (that is, Bethlehem).

Ben-Oni means child of sorrow but his father changed his name to Benjamin which means child of my right hand.

ICHABOD

1 Samuel 4:19-22 KJV

And his (Eli's) daughter in law, Phinehas' wife, was with child, near to be delivered: and when she heard the tidings that the ark of God was taken, and that her father in law and her husband were dead, she bowed herself and travailed; for her pains came upon her. And about the time of her death the women that stood by her said unto her, Fear not; for thou hast born a son. But she answered not, neither did she regard it . And she named the child I-chabod, saying, The glory is departed from Israel: because the ark of God was taken, and because of her father in law and her husband. And she said, The glory is departed from Israel: for the ark of God is taken.

Prophet Eli's daughter in law named the child she died delivering, Ichabod, meaning the glory has departed and truly the glory departed Israel henceforth and it took a long time for the glory to be restored.

JABEZ

1 Chronicles 4:9-10 KJV

And Jabez was more honourable than his brethren: and his mother called his name Jabez, saying, Because I bare him with sorrow. And Jabez called on the God of Israel, saying, Oh that thou wouldest bless me indeed, and enlarge my coast, and that thine hand might be with me, and that thou wouldest keep me from evil, that it may not grieve me! And God granted him that which he requested.

Just like Ben-Oni, born in similar circumstances, his mother named him Jabez, no father was there to change his name like Ben-Oni, until Jabez grew up and decided to do something about his name by praying to God for a change. As long as your name is Ben-Oni or Jabez, sorrow and pain will not be far away.

MOSES

Exodus 2:10 KJV

> And the child grew, and she brought him unto Pharaoh's daughter, and he became her son. And she called his name Moses: and she said, Because I drew him out of the water.

According to the meaning of his name, water played a very significant role in the life of Moses. He was drawn out of water, the biggest obstacle as he led the children of Israel out of Egypt was water because he had to cross over the Red Sea and the menacing army of Pharaoh was pursuing them until God parted the waters of the Red Sea into two. Also, his failure to make it to the promised land had to do with water.

JACOB

Genesis 25:26 KJV

> And after that came his brother out, and his hand took hold on Esau's heel; and his name was called Jacob: and Isaac was threescore years old when she bare them.

Genesis 27:35-36 KJV

> And he said, Thy brother came with deceit,

and hath taken away thy blessing. [36] And he said, Is not he rightly named Jacob? for he hath supplanted me these two times: he took away my birthright; and, behold, now he hath taken away my blessing. And he said, Hast thou not reserved a blessing for me?

Genesis 32:24-28 KJV

And Jacob was left alone; and there wrestled a man with him until the breaking of the day. And when he saw that he prevailed not against him, he touched the hollow of his thigh; and the hollow of Jacob's thigh was out of joint, as he wrestled with him. And he said, Let me go, for the day breaketh. And he said, I will not let thee go, except thou bless me. And he said unto him, What is thy name? And he said, Jacob. And he said, Thy name shall be called no more Jacob, but Israel: for as a prince hast thou power with God and with men, and hast prevailed.

The name of Jacob was like an albatross hanging over his head. Jacob means a trickster or supplanter. He lived true to his name. He lived a crooked life. He supplanted his brother Esau twice before he had an encounter with the Angel of God who changed his name and his destiny received a turn around as well.

NABAL

1 Samuel 25:25 KJV

> [25] Let not my lord, I pray thee, regard this man of Belial, even Nabal: for as his name is , so is he; Nabal is his name, and folly is with him: but I thine handmaid saw not the young men of my lord, whom thou didst send.

Nabal means folly, and as long as his name was Nabal, foolishness was always with him. Indeed he died from his foolish acts!

From these few biblical examples, we can see the significance of a name and for this reason, parent should seek the face of God in prayers for what name to call their child because destiny often follows the names by which an individual is called.

Luke 1:13 KJV

> But the angel said unto him, Fear not, Zacharias: for thy prayer is heard; and thy wife Elisabeth shall bear thee a son, and thou shalt call his name John.

PRAYER POINTS

1. Father, I offer my thanksgiving to you for your mercy in the safe delivery of my new baby.
2. Father, I offer my thanksgiving to you that I am alive to celebrate the delivery of my new baby.
3. Father, I offer thanksgiving to you because you have helped me to deliver a healthy, perfect and normal baby.
4. Father, I offer thanksgiving to you that my baby is not an orphan from birth, that I am alive to nurture my own child by myself.
5. Father, I offer thanksgiving to you for everyone that you used in the process of bringing forth my child including my spouse, doctors, nurses, midwives, and all my loved ones and helpers.
6. Father, I receive divine inspiration for the appropriate, heavenly approved and ordained name for my child.
7. Dear father, you divinely spoke the name of John the baptist to the heart of the parent, please speak to us regarding the name of our child, in the name of Jesus.
8. I denounce and renounce every name that has demonic and idolatrous origin in my father's and mother's lineage, in the name of Jesus.
9. Father, I stand in the gap to pray for sanitization and sanctification of the spiritual origin and

foundation of my family name from my father's and mother's lineage, in the name of Jesus.

10. Father, you changed Abram's name and his destiny responded to his new name as father of nations; Lord, I give you permission to visit the paternal root of my existence and make necessary changes to my name, in the name of Jesus.
11. Father, you changed Sarai's name and her destiny responded immediately as she became the mother of nations; Lord, I give you permission to visit the maternal root of my existence and make necessary changes to my name, in the name of Jesus.
12. Father, you inspired Jacob to change Ben-Oni's name meaning sorrow, to Benjamin, divinely inspire me regarding any name that carries evil connotation in my lineage so I can make the right changes, in Jesus name.
13. The God that answered the prayers of Jabez and gave him a new name, answer my prayers regarding every name in my family that needs your correction, so we can all fulfill great destiny, in the name of Jesus.
14. The God that visited Jacob and changed his name from a crook to a prince, visit me O God where I need a divine visitation. I give you permission to change whatever needs a

change in my spiritual foundation, in the name of Jesus.

15. Father, every name I bear or that my children bear and answer in the realm of the spirit, which is like an albatross, let there be a supernatural change, in the name of Jesus.
16. Father, Nabal's name, meaning foolishness brought him into doing foolish things that ultimately led to his destruction; I disengage myself and my children by force or fire from every any name in my father's or mother's lineage with terrible connotations, in the name of Jesus.
17. I command my children to answer to the prophetic destiny of their names, in the name of Jesus.
18. I command my sons to answer to the prophetic destiny of their names, in the name of Jesus.
19. I command my daughters to answer to the prophetic destiny of their names, in the name of Jesus.
20. The God of Zacharias that inspired the name of John; answer my prayers, I ask for a divine inspiration regarding my expected baby's name, in the name of Jesus.
21. By the name of John, he fulfilled destiny; he became the greatest prophet of his time, by my child's name, he/she shall fulfill destiny and

be the greatest in his/her time, in the name of Jesus.

22. In the name of Jesus, I decree that great accomplishments shall follow the names of my child.
23. Father, I decree that favor shall follow the name of my child, and wherever the name shall be called, heaven will arise and stand at attention to defend, in the name of Jesus.
24. Father, I pray for a supernatural visitation upon every destiny in my family that is answering to the name of Ichabod; let there be a supernatural restoration of every such lost glory, in the name of Jesus.
25. I decree by the power of the Holy Spirit that my child's name shall not be mentioned in jail.
26. I decree by the power of the Holy Spirit that my child's name shall not be mentioned in prison.
27. I decree by the power of the Holy Spirit that my child's name shall not be mentioned in mental asylum.
28. Anytime and anywhere my child's name is mentioned for favor, let heavens arise to bring it to pass, in the name of Jesus.
29. Any gathering and anywhere my child's name is mentioned for evil or disaster, let the God that answers by fire arise, scatter and consume such

gathering, in the name of Jesus.

30. My children's names shall be associated with greatness and godliness in their generation, in the name of Jesus.
31. Father, I thank you for answered prayers. Thank you for a great accomplishment that shall accompany the names of my children, in Jesus name.

CHAPTER 6

CHILDHOOD DISEASE & DEATH: PRAYING AGAINST INFANT MORTALITY

We spend the first 12 months of our children's lives teaching them to walk and talk and the next 12 months teaching them to sit down and shut up.

- Phyllis Diller

ABOUT 29,000 CHILDREN DIE DAILY!

According to United Nations Children's Fund (UNICEF) report, about 29,000 children under the age of five die each day, and that translates to about 21 children every minute! There are 11 million children deaths every year. About 70% of these deaths are attributable to common causes highlighted in previous chapters and by the power of God preventable and treatable. The rest million deaths are attributable to all kinds of causes and situations including those reasons that may defy medical explanations.

As ECM, a non-profit, (Every Child Matters Education Fund) President Michael Petit wrote in a news essay published by the British Broadcasting Corporation.

"Over the past 10 years, more than 20,000 American children are believed to have been killed in their own homes by family members. That is nearly four times the number of US soldiers killed in Iraq and Afghanistan. The child maltreatment death rate in the US is triple Canada's and 11 times that of Italy. Millions of children are reported as abused and neglected every year." (http://www.bbc.co.uk/news/magazine-15193530.)

The issue of infants death due to diseases, sicknesses, satanic operations and other causes have been around since time immemorial. There are few things worse than the death of or arrested development of children. For this reason, parents must devote time to take care of their infants and pray fervently for their infants to live onto childhood and adulthood. There are peculiar childhood diseases and afflictions which truncate the development of children at that age or snatch children away at such age. Some of them have been highlighted above and thank God are preventable and treatable. But we must also recognize that in the spiritual, there are Pharaohs and Herods that Satan raises up to kill children at infancy, just like the time of the birth of Moses in the book of Exodus and the time of the birth of Jesus Christ in Luke.

SCRIPTURES FOR MEDITATION

Exodus 1:16

> So Pharaoh commanded all his people, saying, "Every son who is born you shall cast into the river, and every daughter you shall save alive."

Matthew 2:13,16 KJV

> And when they were departed, behold, the angel of the Lord appeareth to Joseph in a dream, saying, Arise, and take the young child and his mother, and flee into Egypt, and be thou there until I bring thee word: for Herod will seek the young child to destroy him. Then Herod, when he saw that he was mocked of the wise men, was exceeding wroth, and sent forth, and slew all the children that were in Bethlehem, and in all the coasts thereof, from two years old

> and under, according to the time which he had diligently enquired of the wise men.

The birth of Moses.

In **Exodus 1:15-22, 2:1-3,** we see another interesting account of how a heinous and wicked Pharaoh made a decree to kill all male born Hebrews at birth. But by some miraculous intervention and dogged resolve of a mother, her son, Moses was saved at birth, under the same dispensation.

> "Then the king of Egypt spoke to the Hebrew midwives, of whom the name of one was Shiphrah and the name of the other Puah; and he said, "When you do the duties of a midwife for the Hebrew women, and see them on the birthstools, if it is a son, then you shall kill him; but if it is a daughter, then she shall live." But the midwives feared God, and did not do as the king of Egypt commanded them, but saved the male children alive. So the king of Egypt called for the midwives and said to them, "Why have you done this thing, and saved the male children alive?" And the midwives said to Pharaoh, "Because the Hebrew women are not like the Egyptian women; for they are lively and give birth

before the midwives come to them."

So Pharaoh commanded all his people, saying, "Every son who is born you shall cast into the river, and every daughter you shall save alive." **(Exodus 1:15-19, 22 NKJV**)

And a man of the house of Levi went and took as wife a daughter of Levi. So the woman conceived and bore a son. And when she saw that he was a beautiful child, she hid him three months. But when she could no longer hide him, she took an ark of bulrushes for him, daubed it with asphalt and pitch, put the child in it, and laid it in the reeds by the river's bank. And his sister stood afar off, to know what would be done to him. (**Exodus 2:1-4 NKJV)**

MOSES MIRACULOUSLY DELIVERED AT BIRTH

By the decree of Pharaoh, Moses ought to have been killed by the midwife, but God made the midwife to keep him alive. But Pharaoh must not see Moses alive. So, the mother took a brave action. The earthly parents of Jesus took action against the satanic decree of Herod to destroy all newly born males at the birth of Jesus by making sacrifice to go to Egypt as God instructed in order to save their son.

JOCHEBED, MOSES' MOTHER BUILT AN ARK FOR THE SAVING OF HER SON, MOSES

Parents like Jochebed were uncommon in her days. Fathers or mothers who risked their lives to preserve the destiny of their children were rare. In the face of instant death to her son or her own death, she decided bravely and courageously to build an ark for the saving of her son, Moses. She built an ark and put Moses as a baby in it on the Nile, where Moses was miraculously picked up on the river and saved by Pharaoh's daughter. I can envision Jochebed on her knees, crying out to God on behalf of her endangered baby. For this reason, the destiny of a deliverer of a nation was preserved. Jochebed stood out as the only woman that built one of the three arks in the Bible. Noah built one, Moses' mother built one and Moses himself built one. How many mothers are willing to stand up today in the face of possible loss of their lives like Moses' mother? Where was Amram, the father of Moses? The only record in the bible about him in Exodus 6:20 was that he had a wife, had children and died at the age of 137 years. Nothing significant was recorded for posterity about him, while the wife was taking bold action. May the Lord bless all mothers in past and present generations who have stood up boldly and courageously for the preservation of the destiny of their children.

ISHMAEL MIRACULOUSLY DELIVERED FROM DEATH AS A BABY

Genesis 21:14-21 NKJV

"So Abraham rose early in the morning, and took bread and a skin of water; and putting it on her shoulder, he gave it and the boy to Hagar, and sent her away. Then she departed and wandered in the Wilderness of Beersheba. And the water in the skin was used up, and she placed the boy under one of the shrubs. Then she went and sat down across from him at a distance of about a bowshot; for she said to herself, "Let me not see the death of the boy." So she sat opposite him, and lifted her voice and wept. And God heard the voice of the lad. Then the angel of God called to Hagar out of heaven, and said to her, "What ails you, Hagar? Fear not, for God has heard the voice of the lad where he is. Arise, lift up the lad and hold him with your hand, for I will make him a great nation." Then

God opened her eyes, and she saw a well of water. And she went and filled the skin with water, and gave the lad a drink. So God was with the lad; and he grew and dwelt in the wilderness, and became an archer. He dwelt in the Wilderness of Paran; and his mother took a wife for him from the land of Egypt."

BABY JESUS MIRACULOUSLY DELIVERED FROM HEROD'S DESTRUCTION

Matthew 2:13-14,19-20 KJV

"And when they were departed, behold, the angel of the Lord appeareth to Joseph in a dream, saying, Arise, and take the young child and his mother, and flee into Egypt, and be thou there until I bring thee word: for Herod will seek the young child to destroy him. When he arose, he took the young child and his mother by night, and departed into Egypt: But when Herod was dead, behold, an angel of the Lord appeareth in a dream to Joseph in Egypt, Saying, Arise, and take the young child and his mother, and go into the land of Israel: for they are dead which sought the young child's life."

CAREGIVER KILLED FOUR CHILDREN UNDER CARE!

There are several people in Pharaoh and Herod's clothing today, that the devil can use and is using to destroy the lives of innocent children. I pray that our infant children will not be victims in the name of Jesus. Imagine the case of Jessica Tata, a 24-year old children day care operator in Houston Texas who was sentenced to 80 years imprisonment in 2011. Jessica Tata killed four children and severely injured three others below age four when she left them alone to go shopping at a nearby Target Store in February 2011. Fire started from a pan of oil she had left cooking on the stove while she was out. She immediately fled the country to escape arrest and prosecution, but was captured after a month and deported back to the U.S. to face criminal prosecution. The kind of Jessica's Pharaoh and Herod who by their criminal acts would sentence innocent infant children to their untimely grave still abound today in daycare, schools, families etc. for this reason, we must not only be watchful but also prayerful regarding the the hands of such satanic agents over the destiny of our children.

Jeremiah 31:15-17 NKJV

Thus says the LORD: "A voice was heard

in Ramah, Lamentation and bitter weeping, Rachel weeping for her children, Refusing to be comforted for her children, Because they are no more." Thus says the LORD: "Refrain your voice from weeping, And your eyes from tears; For your work shall be rewarded, says the LORD, And they shall come back from the land of the enemy. There is hope in your future, says the LORD, That your children shall come back to their own border."

Mark 9:17-18 KJV

And one of the multitude answered and said, Master, I have brought unto thee my son, which hath a dumb spirit; And wheresoever he taketh him, he teareth him: and he foameth, and gnasheth with his teeth, and pineth away: and I spake to thy disciples that they should cast him out; and they could not.

Exodus 1:22 NKJV

So Pharaoh commanded all his people, saying, "Every son who is born you shall cast into the river, and every daughter you shall save alive."

Exodus 23:26 KJV

There shall nothing cast their young, nor be barren, in thy land: the number of thy days I will fulfill.

ISAIAH 28:18A NKJV

Your covenant with death will be annulled, And your agreement with the grave will not stand.

Psalms 79:11 NKJV

Let the groaning of the prisoner come before You; According to the greatness of Your power Preserve those who are appointed to die.

Psalms 102:19-20 NKJV

For He looked down from the height of His sanctuary; From heaven the LORD viewed the earth, To hear the groaning of the prisoner, To release those appointed to death.

Psalms 91:16 NKJV

With long life I will satisfy him, And show him My salvation."

Psalms 116:16-17 NKJV

The right hand of the LORD is exalted; The right hand of the LORD does valiantly. I shall not die, but live, And declare the works of the LORD.

The purpose of every spiritual Herod's decree is to kill or destroy children of destiny from infancy and to bring sorrow, tears and weeping to their parents. For this reason, prayer against infant mortality through childhood diseases, sicknesses and every other form of attacks must be deliberate and fervent.

PRAYER POINTS

1. Father, I thank you for your mercy to get pregnant and the grace and strength to carry the pregnancy to term.
2. Father, I thank you that I did not suffer abortion, miscarriage or still born of pregnancy
3. Father, I thank you for the opportunity to bring forth a normal and perfect child
4. Father, I thank you for taking me through the danger of child labor and delivery
5. Father, thank you for keeping me alive to experience the joy of being a new mother.
6. Father, I commit the health of my child to you against every form of infant mortality. No infantile affliction shall come upon my child, in Jesus name.
7. My child shall not suffer from any form of childhood disease, in the name of Jesus.
8. Father, I commit the growth of my child unto the supervision of the Holy Spirit, let my child experience normal, perfect and healthy growth and development, in Jesus name.
9. I decree normal mental, physical and spiritual

growth for my child in the name of Jesus.

10. In the name of Jesus, I pray that my child shall not suffer stunted, abnormal, delayed or arrested growth, in the name of Jesus.
11. Holy Spirit, arrest every spiritual arrester of the normal growth of my child, in Jesus name.
12. I pray against every form of truncated growth and development of my child, in the name of Jesus.
13. I come against every retarded growth in speech, in the name of Jesus.
14. I come against every form of delayed development of any organ in my child's body, in Jesus name.
15. I shield my child by the power of the Holy Spirit from every afflicter of children's destiny at daycare center, school and society, in the name of Jesus.
16. It is recorded in the Bible that Jesus Christ grew; my child shall grow in the name of Jesus.
17. It is recorded that the teachers of the law marveled at the intellect of the boy Jesus; let my child become an intellectual amazement to many, in the name of Jesus.
18. From childhood, I put a mark of "touch not" upon my child, in the name of Jesus.
19. No evil hand shall be stretched towards my child nor touch my child, in Jesus name.

20. No evil eye shall behold my child nor his/her destiny, in Jesus name.
21. As it is written, I and the children that you have given unto me are for signs and wonders and so shall it be, in Jesus name.
22. Every tongue that rises up against the destiny of my child, I condemn now by he power of the Holy Spirit, in Jesus name.
23. Spirit of the living God, raise up a standard against every planned satanic assault on my children, in the name of Jesus.
24. I decree death upon every Pharaoh of the destiny of my 'Moses', in Jesus name.
25. I decree death upon every 'Herod' of the destiny of my children, in Jesus name.
26. Holy Ghost, fight every 'Pharaoh' and every 'Herod' of the destiny of my children, in Jesus name.
27. Father, send your angels of deliverance against every 'Herod' of the destiny of my children in Jesus name.
28. Every 'Herod' that is trying to kill or cover the star of my child, receive a death sentence now, in the name of Jesus.
29. Father, as you supernaturally delivered Ishmael from adverse situation of death at infancy, please deliver my child from adverse situation of death, in the name of Jesus.

30. Father, you miraculously preserved the destiny of Ishmael; Lord deliver the destiny of my children from every form of infant mortality, in the name of Jesus.
31. Father, you made provision for the sustenance of the life of Ishmael to the mother; I receive divine provision now for the sustenance of the lives of my children, now in the name of Jesus.
32. Father, you preserved Ishmael; he grew up and took a wife. The destiny of my children shall be preserved; they shall grow up, have their wives and their husbands, and their children, in the name of Jesus.
33. Father, I decree on the authority of your word, a cancellation of every covenant of death hanging over any of my children's destiny, in the name of Jesus.
34. Father I decree on the authority of your word, an annulment of every agreement with the grave over the destiny of any of my children, in the name of Jesus.
35. Father, I decree on the authority of your word, I shall not cast my young, nor bury any of my children, nor know the cemetery of any of my children, in the name of Jesus.
36. Father, I decree on the authority of your word that my children shall live to fulfill the number of their years, in the name of Jesus.

37. Father, I decree that my children shall be accomplished and fulfilled in their lifetime, in the name of Jesus.
38. Father, let your right hand be exalted and prevail valiantly over the destiny of my children, in the name of Jesus.
39. Father, I decree on the authority of your word that my children shall live; they shall not die, in the name of Jesus.
40. Father, I decree on the authority of your word that my children shall live to fulfill the goodness of the Lord, the works of the Lord, and the glory of the Lord, in the name of Jesus.
41. Father, I decree on the authority of your word that none of my children shall face premature death, untimely death, accidental death or sudden death, in the name of Jesus.
42. Father, I decree on the authority of your word that my children shall be satisfied with long life, in the name of Jesus.
43. Father, I thank you for answered prayers.

CHAPTER 7

HEALTHY DEVELOPMENT: PRAYERS FOR PERFECT GROWTH AND DEVELOPMENT

To be in your children's memories tomorrow, you have to be in their lives today."

- Barbara Johnson

Some children come out of the womb normal and healthy but soon after, they begin to manifest evidence of stunted growth and arrested development spiritually, physically, mentally and socially. For this reason, there must be deliberate prayers to fortify our children's growth from every form of satanic attack concerning their development. It becomes a social problem for example, when a child who should have outgrown bed-wetting still bed-wets into teenage years! I have seen the sorrow and sadness in the face of such parents as they come with their children for prayers and God gave them victory. Parents have requested for prayers for their children scoring below 40% in every examination and on every subject in school, thereby bringing sadness and sorrow to the hearts of the parents; parents have come requesting for prayers for children who by age four can hardly open their mouth much less of speaking any word! I have witnessed God given such afflicted children victory through the spiritual efforts of their parents. From every and any form of affliction plaguing any of your children, I decree a total victory, in the name of Jesus.

COMMON INFANT & TODDLER DISEASES

From Center for Diseases Control (CDC):

- Tuberculosis
- Autism spectrum disorders (ASDs)
- Birth Defects
- Cancer
- Cerebral Palsy
- Chickenpox
- Common Cold
- Conjunctivitis (Pink Eye)
- Developmental Disabilities
- Diabetes Prevention

- Diphtheria
- Down Syndrome
- Ear Infection
- Fetal Alcohol Spectrum Disorders (FASDs)
- Flu
- Foodborne Diseases
- Group B Strep
- Hand, Foot and Mouth Disease
- Hearing Loss
- ADHD: Attention Deficit Hyperactivity Disorder
- Neonatal infection
- Hepatitis A
- Hepatitis B
- Hib Disease
- Influenza (Flu)
- Intellectual Disability
- Jaundice (Kernicterus)
- Kernicterus (Jaundice)
- Cold & Cough
- Parasitic Diseases
- Pertussis (Whooping Cough)Pink Eye (Conjunctivitis)
- Recreational Water Illness (RWI)
- Rotavirus
- SIDS
- Sinus Infection
- Sore Throat

- Spina Bifida
- Vision Impairment
- Diarrhea, Cholera
- Polio
- Malaria
- HIV/AIDS

Source: Center for Disease Control (CDC) Report.

SCRIPTURES FOR MEDITATION

1 Samuel 2:18-21

Samuel ministered before the LORD, even as a child, wearing a linen ephod. Moreover his mother used to make him a little robe, and bring it to him year by year when she came up with her husband to offer the yearly sacrifice. And Eli would bless Elkanah and his wife, and say, "The LORD give you descendants from this woman for the loan that was given to the LORD." Then they would go to their own home. And the LORD visited Hannah, so that she conceived and bore three sons and two daughters. Meanwhile the child Samuel grew before the LORD.

Luke 1:80 NKJV

So the child (John) grew and became strong in spirit, and was in the deserts till the day of his manifestation to Israel.

Luke 2:40 NKJV

And the Child (Jesus Christ) grew and became strong in spirit, filled with wisdom; and the grace of God was upon Him.

Luke 2:40, 52 NKJV

And Jesus increased in wisdom and stature, and in favor with God and men.

Luke 2:42,46-47 KJV

And when he was twelve years old, they went up to Jerusalem after the custom of the feast. And it came to pass, that after three days they found him in the temple, sitting in the midst of the doctors, both hearing them, and asking them questions. And all that heard him were astonished at his understanding and answers.

Psalm 119:99 KJV

I have more understanding than all my teachers: for thy testimonies are my meditation.

Galatians 6:17 KJV

From henceforth let no man trouble me: for I bear in my body the marks of the Lord Jesus.

While most of these diseases can be medically explained and treated, there are still cases where the affection upon children have spiritual origin.

CHILDREN SUFFERING FOR THE SINS OF THEIR MOTHER

I once had to minister to a lady who had little children under some strange demonic oppression. The family came and narrated all they had been through regarding the children, and as we prayed, the Holy Spirit spoke to me that the woman had been engaged in adultery . After she got married to the husband, she had engaged in adulterous relationship with two different men at the same time! The word of God cannot be broken according to Ezekiel 18:2: 'the mother has eaten the sour grape and the teeth of the children were set on edge'. That in addition to some other spiritual problems, were the ways the devil had entered into the family to torment the children and the family. She later came to see me by herself, and I asked her if she was ready to confess, repent, forsake her evil ways and make restitution. She did, and God broke the yoke afflicting the children. To the glory of God, the children are free today and doing very well. The woman and her family were rescued from the jaws of physical torment and spiritual death.

PRAYER POINTS

1. Father. I give you praise and thanks for your

mercy bestowed upon my children to see the age of infancy.

2. Father, I give you thanks that my children did not die in the womb or at birth.
3. Father, as my children will be growing up, let them enjoy your mercy on a daily basis, in the name of Jesus.
4. Father, I pray for mercy against anything that could have been done by me or any of my ancestors that could have negative impact on the destiny of my children in the name of Jesus.
5. Father, I pray that none of my children shall suffer for the carelessness, error or sins of mine or my ancestors, in the name of Jesus.
6. Father, I come against every and all form of infant disease against my child. in the name of Jesus.
7. Father, I pray that none of my children shall suffer from common and peculiar infant diseases, in the name of Jesus.
8. Father, shield all my children from every form of specific and strange disease, in the name of Jesus.
9. I decree, in the name of Jesus, that no sickness or disease shall afflict or trouble my children, because they bear upon their body the mark of the Lord Jesus.
10. On the authority of your word, the child Samuel

grew, I decree that my children will grow, in the name of Jesus.

11. On the authority of your word, the child Samuel ministered to the Lord from his childhood years. I decree that my child shall minister and be used of God from childhood years, in the name of Jesus.
12. The favor upon child Samuel opened the doors of fruitfulness and multiplication to the parents. I decree the favor of God that opens the door to fruitfulness and multiplication upon my child, in the name of Jesus.
13. On the authority of your word, the boy John grew and became very strong in the spirit, my children will grow and become very strong in the spirit, in the name of Jesus.
14. On the authority of your word, the destiny of the child John was preserved in a place until the day of his manifestation. I decree a divine preservation for the destiny of my child, in the name of Jesus.
15. Father, on the authority of your word, the child Jesus Christ grew and became very strong in the spirit, I decree growth and spiritual strength for my child, in the name of Jesus.
16. Father, on the authority of your word, the child Jesus Christ was filled with wisdom and the grace of God was upon Him. I pray for

divine wisdom and grace of God to rest upon my child in full measure, in the name of Jesus.

17. Father, on the authority of your word, the child Jesus increased in wisdom and stature; I decree increase in wisdom and stature for my child, in the name of Jesus.
18. Father, on the authority of your word, Jesus increased in favor with God and with men; I pray that my child shall enjoy heavenly and earthly favor, in the name of Jesus.
19. Father, Jesus Christ began to demonstrate uncommon wisdom from childhood; I decree uncommon wisdom upon my child from childhood, in the name of Jesus.
20. Father, I pray for a supernatural endowment of wisdom and understanding upon my child, in the name of Jesus.
21. Father, I decree wisdom, knowledge and understanding that distinguishes and separates children from peers to rest upon my child, in the name of Jesus.
22. Father, fill the heart of my child with your word and by it, grant my child more understanding than his/her teacher, in the name of Jesus.
23. I decree and declare that the growth and development of my children shall not be demonically arrested, in the name of Jesus.
24. I decree and declare that the growth and

development of my children shall not be stunted or arrested by forces of evil, in the name of Jesus.

25. Father, I pray that my child shall develop normally- physically, spiritually, intellectually and socially, in the name of Jesus.
26. Father, I thank you that the destiny of my child is secured and preserved from every form of satanic arrest or harassment, in the name of Jesus.
27. Father, I thank you for answered prayers; blessed be your holy name.

CHAPTER 8

DELIVERANCE & PRAYERS FOR TEENAGE & YOUNG ADULT YEARS

If you bungle raising children, I don't think whatever you do matters very much

- Jackie Kennedy

This phase of life is about the most crucial and critical in a child's development into adulthood. This is the transitory stage where most human beings form their character, behavior, attitude and disposition in life, good or bad. Most of the time, the character formation at this phase of development often determines who an individual turns out to be in adulthood. These are the adventurous and restless years. During this phase, children take a lot of risks, some of which are life threatening and others are positively life impacting. For this reason, parents must be deliberate and dedicated to the development and safety of their children. We will look at the negative character formation in this chapter and the good character formation in the next chapter with relevant examples and appropriate prayers. One important thing we must not fail to do for our children at this stage of life is to train them. The scripture says "Train up a child in the way he should go, And when he is old he will not depart from it." **(Proverbs 22:6 NKJV)**

THE PARENTING STYLE OF JACOB & JESSE

The bible says parents must train up the child in the way of the Lord, so there is a responsibility, both physical and spiritual, on the part of the parent for the upbringing of a child. Jacob, Joseph's father, loved him so much more than his brothers, being the son of his old age, he made a coat of many colors for him only. That was favoritism of one child over another. The coat of many colors led to sibling rivalry and hatred that almost cost Joseph his life in the hands of his envious brothers. Jacob's parenting style was questionable here. However, Jesse, David's father sent him to be tending to the flock by himself as a child, the youngest among eight brothers, and thereby teaching him the value of hard work and discipline which experience later paid off for him handsomely in confronting Goliath. That was good parenting on the part of Jesse.

There are typical childhood and teenage years phenomena, behaviors, lifestyle, dangers and risks, especially in the present generation. Some of them include:

- Peer pressure
- Good and bad choices
- Sibling rivalries
- Destitution and vagabond spirit.
- Good and bad company, friendship and association.

Life threatening and risky adventures: hazing, gang, risky and illegal activities like car racing, dragging, over speeding etc.

Good and destructive behavior: disciplined culture, obedient spirit, rebellious spirit, disobedient spirit, indiscipline, laziness, etc.

Strange appetite and destructive addiction and risky adventures like drug, nicotine and smoking, liquor, alcohol experimentation, indecent appearance, sexual perversion, etc

Destructive lifestyle: Wild partying, revelry, recreational sex, pornography, etc.

Prodigal spirit: wastefulness of time, resource and opportunity.

Lack of self motivation, layback attitude, indifference attitude to important issues of life, etc.

SAMSON'S PARENTS' SPIRITUAL INSENSITIVITY

Judges 14:3-4 NKJV

> Then his father and mother said to him, "Is there no woman among the daughters of your brethren, or among all my people, that you must go and get a wife from the uncircumcised Philistines?" And Samson said to his father, "Get her for me, for she pleases me well." But his father and mother did not know that it was of the LORD—that He was seeking an occasion to move against the Philistines. For at that time the Philistines had dominion over Israel.

The spiritual insensitivity of Samson's parents contributed significantly to the truncation of his destiny, leading to the pathetic and premature demise of Samson. Despite God's instructions regarding his upbringing before he was born, the parents did not do what was expected as godly parents in order for him to fulfill his God-given destiny in a glorious way.

SCRIPTURES FOR MEDITATION

Isaiah 44:3 NKJV

"For I will pour water on him who is thirsty, And floods on the dry ground; I will pour My Spirit on your descendants, And My blessing on your offspring."

Jeremiah 31:15-17 NKJV

Thus says the LORD: "A voice was heard in Ramah, Lamentation and bitter weeping, Rachel weeping for her children, Refusing to be comforted for her children, Because they are no more." Thus says the LORD: "Refrain your voice from weeping, And your eyes from tears; For your work shall be rewarded, says the LORD, And they shall come back from the land of the enemy. There is hope in your future, says the LORD, That your children shall come back to their own border.

Genesis 18:19 KJV

For I know him, that he will command his children and his household after him, and they shall keep the way of the Lord , to do justice and judgment; that the Lord may bring upon Abraham that which he hath spoken of him.

Malachi 2:15 KJV

And did not he make one? Yet had he the

residue of the spirit. And wherefore one? That he might seek a godly seed. Therefore take heed to your spirit, and let none deal treacherously against the wife of his youth.

Psalms 144:7-8, 11-12 KJV

Send thine hand from above; rid me, and deliver me out of great waters, from the hand of strange children; Whose mouth speaketh vanity, and their right hand is a right hand of falsehood.

Rid me, and deliver me from the hand of strange children, whose mouth speaketh vanity, and their right hand is a right hand of falsehood: That our sons may be as plants grown up in their youth; that our daughters may be as corner stones, polished after the similitude of a palace:

Proverbs 22:6 KJV

Train up a child in the way he should go: and when he is old, he will not depart from it.

Genesis 37:3-4 KJV

Now Israel loved Joseph more than all his children, because he was the son of his old age: and he made him a coat of many colors. And when his brethren saw that their father loved him more than all his brethren, they hated him, and could not speak peaceably unto him.

1 Samuel 16:11 KJV

> And Samuel said unto Jesse, Are here all thy children? And he said, There remaineth yet the youngest, and, behold, he keepeth the sheep. And Samuel said unto Jesse, Send and fetch him: for we will not sit down till he come hither.

YOUNG ADULT YEARS EVIL ATTACKS

There are some examples of individual youths who fell victims of these malaise in the bible:

1. Children Of Adam (Cain & Abel): Hatred, Murder

Genesis 4:1-9 KJV

And Adam knew Eve his wife; and she conceived, and bare Cain, and said, I have gotten a man from the Lord . And she again bare his brother Abel. And Abel was a keeper of sheep, but Cain was a tiller of the ground. And in process of time it came to pass, that Cain brought of the fruit of the ground an offering unto the Lord. And Abel, he also brought of the firstlings of his flock and of the fat thereof. And the Lord had respect unto Abel and to his offering: But unto Cain and to his offering he had not respect. And Cain was very wroth, and his countenance fell. [6] And the Lord said unto Cain, Why art thou wroth? and why is thy countenance fallen? If thou doest well, shalt thou not be accepted? and if thou doest not well, sin lieth at the door. And unto thee shall be his desire, and thou shalt rule over him. And Cain talked with Abel his brother: and it came to pass, when they were in the field, that Cain rose up against Abel his brother, and slew him. And the Lord said unto Cain, Where is Abel thy brother? And he said, I know not: Am I my brother's keeper?

Here, Cain committed the first recorded murder in the bible against his own brother, due to envy and wrath.

2. Jacob's Children: Hatred, Envy, Indiscipline

Genesis 37:3-4 KJV (HATRED)

> [3] Now Israel loved Joseph more than all his children, because he was the son of his old age: and he made him a coat of many colours. [4] And when his brethren saw that their father loved him more than all his brethren, they hated him, and could not speak peaceably unto him.

Genesis 37:11,18 KJV (ENVY)

> And his brethren envied him; but his father observed the saying. And when they saw him afar off, even before he came near unto them, they conspired against him to

slay him.

Here, we see the first recorded offense of conspiracy to commit a crime in the bible, where siblings were the culprits.

Genesis 49:3-4 KJV (INDISCIPLINE)

Reuben, thou art my firstborn, my might, and the beginning of my strength, the excellency of dignity, and the excellency of power: Unstable as water, thou shalt not excel; because thou wentest up to thy father's bed; then defiledst thou it : he went up to my couch.

3. Dinah: Incident Adventure, Peer Pressure & Rape

Genesis 34:1-2,7 KJV

And Dinah the daughter of Leah, which she bare unto Jacob, went out to see the daughters of the land. And when Shechem the son of Hamor the Hivite, prince of the country, saw her, he took her, and lay with her, and defiled her. And the sons of Jacob came out of the field when they heard it : and the men were grieved, and they were very wroth, because he had wrought folly in Israel in lying with Jacob's daughter; which thing ought not to be done.

4. Children Of Prophet Eli: Sexual Abuse 1 Samuel 2:22-24 KJV

Now Eli was very old, and heard all that his sons did unto all Israel; and how they lay with the women that assembled at the door of the tabernacle of the congregation. And he said unto them, Why do ye such things? for I hear of your evil dealings by all this people. Nay, my sons; for it is no good report that I hear: ye make the Lord's people to transgress.

5. Samuel's Children: Dishonest & Corrupt

1 Samuel 8:1,3 KJV

And it came to pass, when Samuel was old, that he made his sons judges over Israel. And his sons walked not in his ways, but turned aside after dishonest gain, and took bribes, and perverted judgment.

6. Amnon And Tamar: Incident, Perverse Behavior: Rape & Incest

2 Samuel 13:14-17 KJV

Howbeit he Amnon would not hearken unto her Tamar's voice: but, being stronger than she, forced her, and lay with her. Then Amnon hated her exceedingly; so that the hatred wherewith he hated her was greater than the love wherewith he had loved her. And Amnon said unto her, Arise, be gone. And she said unto him, There is no cause: this evil in sending me away is greater than the other that thou didst unto me. But he would not hearken unto her.

7. Jonadab And Amnon: Bad Company, Friendship & Association

2 Samuel 13:1-3,5 KJV

> And it came to pass after this, that Absalom the son of David had a fair sister, whose name was Tamar; and Amnon the son of David loved her. And Amnon was so vexed, that he fell sick for his sister Tamar; for she was a virgin; and Amnon thought it hard for him to do any thing to her. But Amnon had a friend, whose name was Jonadab, the son of Shimeah David's brother: and Jonadab was a very crafty man. [5] And Jonadab said unto him, Lay thee down on thy bed, and make thyself sick: and when thy father cometh to see thee, say unto him, I pray thee, let my sister Tamar come, and give me meat, and dress the meat in my sight, that I may see it , and eat it at her hand.

8. Rascally & Disrespectful Behavior
2 Kings 2:23-24 KJV

And he went up from thence unto Beth-el: and as he was going up by the way, there came forth little children out of the city, and mocked him, and said unto him, Go up, thou bald head; go up, thou bald head. And he turned back, and looked on them, and cursed them in the name of the Lord . And there came forth two she bears out of the wood, and tare forty and two children of them.

9. Samson: Strange Appetite & Destructive Lifestyle
Judges 14:1-2 KJV

And Samson went down to Timnath, and saw a woman in Timnath of the daughters of the Philistines. And he came up, and told his father and his mother, and said, I have seen a woman in Timnath of the daughters of the Philistines: now therefore get her for me to wife.

Judges 16:1,4 KJV

Then went Samson to Gaza, and saw there an harlot, and went in unto her. And it came to pass afterward, that he loved a woman in the valley of Sorek, whose name was Delilah.

10. Vagabond Spirit
Jeremiah 31:15-17 (NKJV)

Thus says the LORD: "A voice was heard in Ramah, Lamentation and bitter weeping, Rachel weeping for her children, Refusing to be comforted for her children, Because they are no more." Thus says the LORD: "Refrain your voice from weeping, And your eyes from tears; For your work shall be rewarded, says the LORD, And they shall come back from the land of the enemy. There is hope in your future, says the LORD, That your children shall come back to their own border.

11. Prodigal Spirit.
Luke 15:11-13 KJV

And he said, A certain man had two sons: And the younger of them said to his father, Father, give me the portion of goods that falleth to me . And he divided unto them his living.
And not many days after the younger son gathered all together, and took his journey into a far country, and there wasted his substance with riotous living.

OTHER SCRIPTURES FOR MEDITATION

Proverbs 22:15 KJV

Foolishness is bound in the heart of a child; but the rod of correction shall drive it far from him.

Ecclesiastes 12:1 KJV

Remember now thy Creator in the days of thy youth, while the evil days come not, nor the years draw nigh, when thou shalt say, I have no pleasure in them;

Isaiah 8:18 KJV

Behold, I and the children whom the Lord hath given me are for signs and for wonders in Israel from the Lord of hosts, which dwelleth in mount Zion.

Isaiah 54:13 KJV

And all thy children shall be taught of the Lord ; and great shall be the peace of thy children.

1 Timothy 4:12 KJV

Let no man despise thy youth; but be thou an example of the believers, in word, in conversation, in charity, in spirit, in faith, in purity.

SUFFERING FROM AFFLUENZA: TEENAGER KILLED FOUR PEOPLE AND PARALYZED TWO IN DRUNK DRIVING CAR ACCIDENT!

Ethan Couch is a Burleson, Texas, teenager who at the age of 16 killed four people and paralyzed two others when he caused an accident with his truck while driving drunk. The defense psychologist said at trial that the boy was suffering from a disease called 'affluenza.' According to him, Ethan was a product of wealthy and privileged parents who never set limits or boundaries for their child. Affluenza is a social disease that allows a kid to get away with anything because of their wealthy and privileged parentage. He was given 10 years probation in 2014 instead of 20 years imprisonment. Many children are suffering from 'affluenza' today! Generally, a child that fails to take personal responsibility grows up to become other people's liability. I have seen many parents waste their hard earned income bailing out their unruly children from all kinds of criminal matters. I have seen such parents' predicaments and anguish, and it breaks my heart each time. Satan has turned such children into devourers to their parents.

SON (23), BRUTALLY MURDERED FATHER

News broke in June of 2014 of the cruel killing of a law school classmate of mine, who was also a Pastor. He was brutally murdered by his own son, and this shocked not a few of us. The son who was a 23 years old and in his third year of a bachelor's degree program in the University said he felt offended and upset by the father bordering him about joining him for prayer and going to church. While he was alone with the father, he took a knife and stabbed the father several times. After he made sure he had dead, he cut his dead body to pieces. He put the remains in a sack and put into a wheel-barrow and dumped it in a bush near their home. He came back to their house, sat down and was watching TV! He told those who came to check on his father that he had gone out, until the body was discovered and the marks left by the wheel barrow tires were traced to their home. During police interrogation, he owned up to killing the father, and all he could say was that he apologized for killing his father who had been his benefactor, and to the mother who not now had become a sudden widow, but will also have to live with a son in prison for the rest of her life! The question on the lips of everyone was: "Why must this kind of heinous crime be committed by a son on a father who had struggled practically through life?" The young man confessed he had been doing drugs and of course, must have been a gang member.

ABODE IN STRANGE PLACES

This is the age when some go into destitution, prostitution, evil addiction, etc. There is a pathetic story of a God-fearing family whose child was under this evil affliction from her teenage years. She would not just want to stay in the comfortable home of the parents, but rather, preferred to 'hang out' and sleep about in friend's houses. Little did the parents realize then that it was a spiritual problem. Then she graduated from high school and vanished completely from the house and community where she was much loved and cared for. Nobody could just trace her whereabouts, but she was not missing, because once in a while she would call the parents, and would tell them that she was fine. But the truth was that she was living in places that brought depression of heart to the parents. It brought embarrassment, pain, anguish, sorrows of heart to this responsible family, because they could afford to give her a good life but she rejected the offer. Every spiritually discerning person would know this was not ordinary. The hand of the "world" was manipulating her destiny.

I MUST FIND THE PICTURE AT ALL COST!" SPIRIT OF VAGABOND

Sometime ago, I was speaking in a church and some people came out for some specific ministration. There was a lady who was having a picture of a young man in her hand for me to touch and pray over. Immediately she opened her hand, the Holy Spirit spoke to me that the destiny of the young man in the picture was troubled. I told her to see me regarding the young man. When she came, I told her what the Holy Spirit ministered to me concerning his destiny. She confirmed it was true and that he had been living on the streets of New York for some years now, despite the fact that he had people who could take good care of him. So I asked her to bring the picture for prayers, but all of a sudden, she could not just find the picture. She looked everywhere, went inside the sanctuary, asked the ushers but could not just find it. I told her not to worry that she should just write down his name for me and we would agree in prayer over him. But the lady said, 'sir, I have to get this picture for you.' I wondered why she was so bent on finding the picture. Then she said, 'you don't understand sir; this is the second time that a man of God would request for his picture and all of a sudden the picture would disappear.' Immediately, the Holy Spirit put the matter in spiritual perspective for me, that his destiny was conforming to the demonic spirit of wandering, never to be seen or found where his deliverance is waiting for him, and that is why he has become physically elusive for the family to rehabilitate. She later found the picture and we prayed over it and believed God that urgently, his wandering destiny would find a safe harbor and return home.

PRAYER POINTS

1. Father, I thank you for preserving my children to see their teenage years. Thank you because they did not become fatherless or motherless children at infancy.
2. Father, I thank you for blessing my children with good health through babyhood, infancy to their teenage years.
3. Father, thank you for preserving me to see their teenage and young adult years in good health.
4. Father, I pray for your mercy over my children concerning every mistake of their teenage and adolescent years, in the name of Jesus.
5. Father, forgive the sins of their teenage years, let it not speak against their future, in the name of Jesus.
6. Dear Heavenly Father, help me not to weep over any of my children, in the name of Jesus.
7. Father, I come against every voice of

lamentation and bitter weeping. I shall not shed tears over any of my children, in the name of Jesus.

8. Father, I pray for your supernatural touch over the destiny and future of my children, in the name of Jesus.
9. Dear heavenly father, I pray that you reward my work, efforts, labor and perspiration over my children, in the name of Jesus.
10. Father, in whatever way my child or any of my children have strayed into the camp of the enemy, I called back their destiny now, in the name of Jesus.
11. On the authority of your word, I decree a return of my children to their godly inheritance, in the name of Jesus.
12. I decree that my children shall possess their inheritance, and every plan of the devil to disinherit or dispossess them, is hereby destroyed now, in the name of Jesus.
13. Father, you helped Abraham to command his family in the way of the Lord; help me to command my children in the way of the Lord, in Jesus name.
14. Father, give me godly wisdom to instruct my children in your way, in the name of Jesus.
15. Father, I receive the divine assistance of the Holy Spirit and wisdom to train my children,

instruct them, discipline them, and love them, in Jesus name.

16. Father, as I command my children in the way of the Lord, they will listen, and they will obey, in the name of Jesus.
17. Father, I know and believe that you have given me godly children. I decree that all my children shall live godly lives, in the name of Jesus.
18. Father, according to Psalm 114:7, send thine hand from above to rid and deliver my children from the hand of strange children who speak vanity and practice falsehood, in the name of Jesus.
19. Father, on the authority of your word, I declare that our sons will be as plants grown up in their youth; that our daughters may be as corner stones, polished after the similitude of a palace, in the name of Jesus.
20. Father, I shield the destiny of my children by the power of the Holy Spirit from every influence of strange children, in the name of Jesus.
21. Father, I pray that no one will sabotage the destiny of my children, in the name of Jesus.
22. Father, I pray that my children shall not stray into the camp of the enemy like Dinah, in the name of Jesus.
23. Father, I pray that my daughter shall not fall

victim to sexual abuser and sexual pervert, in the name of Jesus.

24. Father, shield the destiny of my children from every negative peer pressure and the desire to follow the multitude, in the name of Jesus.
25. 25. Father, I pray that none of my children shall turn out to be deviant, destitute, unruly, disobedient, vagabond, rebel, drug addict, sexual abuser, etc, in the name of Jesus.
26. Father, I decree your Spirit to rest upon my children, in the name of Jesus.
27. Father, I pray that my children shall not be afflicted by the spirit of sexual perversion like the children of prophet Eli, in the name of Jesus.
28. Father, I pray that none of my children shall engage in blasphemous conduct like the children of prophet Eli, in the name of Jesus.
29. Father, I envelope the minds of my children in the power of the Holy Spirit, against every form of corruption and compromise, like the children of Samuel, in Jesus name.
30. Father, I pray that none of my children shall be victim or subject of sexual abuse, rape, incest or any other form of sexual perversion, in the name of Jesus.
31. Father, I shield the destiny of my children from every form of bad company, bad association

and bad friendship, in Jesus name.

32. Father, I pray that my children shall not come under negative influences and terrible companies and associations, in Jesus name.
33. I shield the destiny of my children from every form of rascally behavior, disorderly and disrespectful behaviors, in the name of Jesus.
34. Father, Please protect the destiny of my children from reckless or disrespectful behavior that could lead to curses, in Jesus name.
35. By the power of the Holy Spirit, I cover the destiny of my children from every form of strange appetite, and destructive lifestyle that can truncate or destroy their present and their future in Jesus name.
36. Father, by the power of the Holy Spirit, I protect the destiny of my children from every form of rebellious spirit, in the name of Jesus. I pray that my children shall not be rebellious to parents or authorities, in the name of Jesus.
37. Father, by the power of the Holy Spirit, I protect the destiny of my children from every form of prodigal spirit, in the name of Jesus. The spirit that squanders possession shall not afflict any of my children, in Jesus name.
38. In the name of Jesus, I terminate the operation of any and every negative spirit that may be troubling any of my children now, in the name

of Jesus.

39. I decree God's mighty hand upon my children against every form of teenage years common terrible conduct, in the name of Jesus.
40. I decree that by the power of the Holy Spirit, none of my children shall engage in gang activities, risky and illegal conduct, activities and enterprise, illicit drug usage, liquor addiction, nicotine addiction, revelry, wild partying, indecent appearance, prostitution, illicit sexual conduct, bible condemning sexual orientation, conduct and lifestyle, in the name of Jesus.
41. Father, I pray that nobody shall despise or dishonor the youthful years of my children, in the name of Jesus.
42. Father, I pray that my children shall know the Lord, love the Lord, and serve the Lord from their youthful years, in the name of Jesus.
43. Father, I pray that all my children shall be good examples of believers in their conduct, behavior, attitude and activities, in the name of Jesus.
44. Father, I pray that my children shall follow good examples and not terrible ones in their generation, in the name of Jesus.
45. Father, I pray that my children shall set good examples, and not terrible ones in their generation, in the name of Jesus.

46. Father, on the authority of your word, I decree that I and the children you have given to me shall be for great signs and great wonders in our generation, in the name of Jesus.
47. Father, as I teach my children in the way of the Lord, I pray that none of my children shall depart from it, in the name of Jesus.
48. I pray for love among and between my children as siblings. Let them grow up to love each other, in the name of Jesus.
49. I come against every spirit of envy, hatred and every form of sibling rivalry among and between my children, in the name of Jesus. This shall not happen, in Jesus name.
50. Father, I pray on the authority of your word, all my children shall be taught by the Lord and great shall be the peace of all my children, in Jesus name.
51. Father, you are the wisest teacher, teach my children good conduct, appropriate behavior, right attitude, excellent character, in the name of Jesus.
52. Father, I pray that all my children shall give me peace of mind, joyful and pleasant memories in my latter days, in the name of Jesus.
53. Father, I thank you for answered prayers. Thank you because the destiny of my children is secure in Christ and Christ in God, in the name of Jesus.

CHAPTER 9

YOUNG ADULT YEARS EXCELLENCE: PRAYERS FOR ESTABLISHMENT & GRACE

If you raise your children to feel that they can accomplish any goal or task they decide upon, you will have succeeded as a parent and you will have given your children the greatest of all blessings.

- Brian Tracy

This phase is transitory to young adulthood. It is the age of entering into legal maturity. It is the destiny transformation and establishment phase. It's at this stage that crucial long term decisions are made. Such decisions include: choice of career, choice of life partner in marriage. By this stage, character, behavior and personality traits are already formed and individuals start to live them out. People begin to put a permanent description, label or identity upon individuals, good or bad. This is also the stage of legal accountability, when society starts holding individuals legally responsible for their decisions and choices and awards appropriate legal commendation and or legal sanction or condemnation as the case may be. More importantly, this is the age when most great destiny begins to show forth witty inventions and ground breaking ideas in every generation. It is the age of commencement of great exploits in every sphere of life. This was the age when Joseph, Esther, David, Daniel, Shadrach, Meshach, and Abednego, began to accomplish destinies and fulfill prophecies in their generation. It is the same with the present generation.

We have had major scientific and technological breakthroughs from this age group in the present generation. For these reasons, the prayers of parents upon children must be consistent, persistent and intensified. One very important prayer parents must not fail to pray for their children at this stage is for His spirit, His grace and His divine establishment. That God would release his grace upon them and establish the work of their hands. When God establishes the works of their hands and blesses our children, He has also established the works of our hands as parents. Our children are a crucial part of the works of our hands.

As there are numerous examples of bad children in the bible, so are innumerable examples of godly children, who modeled uncommon wisdom, godly characters and virtues, and did great exploits. Some of them include Isaac, Rebeccah, Joseph, Esther, Daniel, Timothy, etc. Common attributes they possessed without exemption is one of the spirits or a combination of some of the spirits that were prophetically released upon Jesus Christ before He was born.

YOUNG AND SUCCESSFUL PEOPLE OF PRESENT GENERATION

Just like the biblical times, there are young people, majority of them under the age of 30, who have made significant contributions in technology in our present generation, through witty inventions, hard work and perseverance.

- **Evan Spiegel** at 24 became the founder and Chief Executive Officer of Snapchat, a photo messaging application. The company is estimated to worth $10 billion, and Evan himself is worth about $1.5 billion.

- **Mark Zuckerberg**, at 23 founded Facebook, the biggest social network company in the world, that is valued at $230 billion (March 2015). Mark at 29 today, is has an estimated net worth of about $34 billion.

- **Dustin Moskovitz** at 29, is co-founder of Facebook, the biggest social network company. Dustin himself has an estimated net worth of about $7 billion.

- **Bill Gates** was in his twenties when he founded Microsoft Corporation, the biggest computer software company in the world. Steve Jobs was in his twenties when he founded Apple Computers, the biggest company in the world today in terms of net worth, valued at $710 billion (February 2015). Larry Page and Sergei Brin, co founders of Google corporation were in their twenties when they founded Google corporation, that is valued at $368 billion (May 2015). Michael Dell founded Dell computers at the age of 27 and Elon Musk at 28 started PayPal, which he later sold to Ebay for $1.5 billion. These are just a few of young people who have redefined the landscape of technology in our present generation through their creativity, innovations and inventions. May the Lord release upon our children the spirit for witty inventions, in

Jesus name.

SCRIPTURES FOR MEDITATION

Psalm 90:17 KJV

And let the beauty of the Lord our God be upon us: and establish thou the work of our hands upon us; yea, the work of our hands establish thou it.

Isaiah 11:1-3 KJV

And there shall come forth a rod out of the stem of Jesse, and a Branch shall grow out of his roots: [2] And the spirit of the Lord shall rest upon him, the spirit of wisdom and understanding, the spirit of counsel and might, the spirit of knowledge and of the fear of the Lord ; And shall make him of quick understanding in the fear of the Lord : and he shall not judge after the sight of his eyes, neither reprove after the hearing of his ears:

- The spirit of the Lord
- The spirit of Wisdom
- The spirit of Understanding
- The spirit of Counsel
- The spirit of Might
- The spirit of Knowledge
- The spirit of Godly Fear

1. Isaac: Obedience

Genesis 22:6 KJV

And Abraham took the wood of the burnt offering, and laid it upon Isaac his son; and he took the fire in his hand, and a knife; and they went both of them together.

2. Rebecca: Courteous and Kind

Genesis 24:45-46 KJV

And before I had done speaking in mine heart, behold, Rebekah came forth with her pitcher on her shoulder; and she went down unto the well, and drew water : and I said unto her, Let me drink, I pray thee. And she made haste, and let down her pitcher from her shoulder , and said, Drink, and I will give thy camels drink also: so I drank, and she made the camels drink also.

3. Daniel, Shadrach, Meshach And Abednego: Discipline, Good Choices, Excellent Spirit

Daniel 1:8 KJV

But Daniel purposed in his heart that he would not defile himself with the portion of the king's meat, nor with the wine which he drank: therefore he requested of the prince of the eunuchs that he might not defile himself.

Daniel 3:17-18 KJV

If it be so , our God whom we serve is able to deliver us from the burning fiery furnace, and he will deliver us out of thine hand, O king. But if not, be it known unto thee, O king, that we will not serve thy gods, nor worship the golden image which thou hast set up.

Daniel 6:3 KJV

Then this Daniel distinguished himself above the presidents and princes, because an excellent spirit was in him; and the king thought to set him over the whole realm.

4. Esther: Chastity, Obedience & Determination

Esther 2:17,20 KJV

And the king loved Esther above all the women, and she obtained grace and favour in his sight more than all the virgins; so that he set the royal crown upon her head, and made her queen instead of Vashti. Esther had not yet shewed her kindred nor her people; as Mordecai had charged her: for Esther did the commandment of Mordecai, like as when she was brought up with him.

Esther 4:16 KJV

Go, gather together all the Jews that are present in Shushan, and fast ye for me, and neither eat nor drink three days, night or day: I also and my maidens will fast likewise; and so will I go in unto the king, which is not according to the law: and if I perish, I perish.

5. The Rechabites: Obedience & Discipline

Jeremiah 35:8-10 KJV

Thus have we obeyed the voice of Jonadab the son of Rechab our father in all that he hath charged us, to drink no wine all our days, we, our wives, our sons, nor our daughters; Nor to build houses for us to dwell in: neither have we vineyard, nor field, nor seed: But we have dwelt in tents, and have obeyed, and done according to all that Jonadab our father commanded us.

Jeremiah 35:18-19 KJV

And Jeremiah said unto the house of the Rechabites, Thus saith the Lord of hosts, the God of Israel; Because ye have obeyed the commandment of Jonadab your father, and kept all his precepts, and done according unto all that he hath commanded you: Therefore thus saith the Lord of hosts, the God of Israel; Jonadab the son of Rechab shall not want a man to stand before me for ever.

6. Timothy: Devotion From Childhood
2 Timothy 3:15 KJV

And that from a child thou hast known the holy scriptures, which are able to make thee wise unto salvation through faith which is in Christ Jesus.

PRAYER POINTS

1. God, I give you praise for who you have been in the life of my children.
2. God, I give you thanks for what you have done in the life of my children.
3. Father, I thank you for preserving my child from infancy to teenage years and to young adulthood.
4. Father, I thank you for not allowing the devil to mess up the destiny of my children.
5. Father, I thank you for not allowing my children to become victims of societal ills and problems.
6. Father, I thank you for preserving the spirit, soul and body of my children from all forms of satanic corruption and ungodly influence,

in Jesus name.

7. Father, thank you for your mercy upon my children regarding their errors and sins, in the name of Jesus.
8. On the authority of your word, I decree the spirit of the Lord to come upon my children, in the name of Jesus.
9. On the authority of your word, I decree the spirit of wisdom to come upon my children, in the name of Jesus.
10. On the authority of your word, I decree the spirit of understanding to come upon my children, in the name of Jesus.
11. On the authority of your word, I decree the spirit of counsel to come upon my children, in Jesus name.
12. On the authority of your word, I decree the spirit of might upon my children, in the name of Jesus.
13. On the authority of your word, I decree the spirit of knowledge and witty inventions to come upon my children, in the name of Jesus.
14. On the authority of your word, I decree the spirit of discernment to come upon my children, in the name of Jesus.
15. On the authority of your word, I decree the spirit of the fear of the Lord to come upon my children, in Jesus name.

16. Father, on the authority of your word, as my children fear the Lord, let this mark the beginning of wisdom and knowledge for them, in the name of Jesus.
17. Father, I pray the spirit of submission and respect that rested upon Isaac to rest upon my children, in Jesus name.
18. Father, the courtesy and kindness of Rebecca attracted your favor upon her, cause my children to experience favor as they demonstrate courtesy and kindness, in Jesus name.
19. Father, I pray that you cause my children to make choices that will bring glory to you like Daniel, in the name of Jesus.
20. Father, I pray your Spirit to cause my children to walk in your precept, like Daniel, and never to compromise with the world, in the name of Jesus.
21. Father, you emboldened Daniel to face a heinous king with courage, release a courageous spirit upon my children to face any adverse situation with boldness, in the name of Jesus.
22. I come against every spirit of defilement and compromise with the world concerning my children, in the name of Jesus.
23. Father, I pray that my children will not serve idols nor worship any image, in the name of Jesus.

24. The destiny of my children shall not suffer a defilement, in the name of Jesus.
25. Father, by your power, you supernaturally delivered Daniel from every persecution he faced for standing for you; deliver my children like Daniel from every persecution for righteousness sake in Jesus name.
26. Father, you preserved the destiny of Daniel from Nebuchadnezzar's lion, preserve the destiny of my children from every roaring lion, in the name of Jesus.
27. Father, you released excellent spirit upon Daniel; he distinguished himself amongst his peers in his generation. Release your excellent spirit upon my children to excel in their generation, in Jesus name.
28. I decree excellent spirit upon my children; let them be distinguished for good and greatness in their generation, in the name of Jesus.
29. Father, Daniel knew his God, he did great exploits in his generation; let the revelation of who you are rest upon my children. Cause them to do greater exploits in their generation, in Jesus name.
30. Joseph stood up for righteousness in his generation and he obtained favor from God, and was successful. Cause a righteous spirit to rest upon my children, and cause them to

succeed in all spheres of life, in Jesus name.

31. Father, by your grace, favor and power, Esther lived a life of chastity, obedience and determination in her generation; cause your grace and power to come upon my children to do exploits in their generation, in the name of Jesus.
32. Father, Esther obtained the favor of the highest authority in her generation; cause my children to enjoy the favor of God and the favor of highest authorities in their generation, in Jesus name.
33. Father, you preserved the destiny of Esther; she did not perish for taking a righteous stand for God. Preserve the destiny of my children from every satanic ambush and snare, in Jesus name.
34. Father, by the obedience of the Rechabites to the instruction passed down to them by their grandfather, you made an everlasting covenant with them and created an everlasting inheritance for them. Cause the spirit of obedience to parental instruction to rest upon my children and their seed, in the name of Jesus.
35. Father, I address and command the spirit of my children to know God and the holy scriptures like Timothy, in the name of Jesus.
36. Father, Isaac, Joseph, Esther, Daniel, Timothy

grew up to be successful adults, cause my children to grow up into successful adults, in the name of Jesus.

37. Father, as my children apply their hearts to know you and love you and your word, cause your wisdom to rest mightily upon them, in Jesus name.
38. Father, as my children begin to make destiny-impacting decisions at this stage of their life, guide them by your spirit; instruct them by your counsel, in the name of Jesus.
39. Father, I pray that in crucial decisions of life, you would help my children to choose within and not outside of your will, in Jesus name.
40. Father, I pray that none of my children's decisions will bring them regret, disappointment or failure, in the name of Jesus.
41. Father, on the authority of your word in Psalm 47:4, choose the inheritance of my children for them, in the name of Jesus.
42. Father, on the authority of your word in Psalm 90:7, let your beauty be upon all my children and establish the works of their hands in Jesus name.
43. Father, I thank you for answering my prayers and petitions over the destiny of my children, in Jesus name.
44. Father, I thank you for the bountiful testimonies

that shall accompany my spiritual exercise over my children, in Jesus name.

CONCLUSION

I want to congratulate you for this exercise of laying a strong spiritual foundation for your children. I pray that their destinies shall respond positively to every word of your prayers over them, in Jesus name. I want to encourage you to take additional step for continuous intercession for their divine establishment in adulthood by using the second volume of this handbook to continue to pray for your offspring. As you continue in prayers for your children and grandchildren in accordance with the word of God, you will live to see the result of your travails in prayers over them, in Jesus name. According to the word of Jesus, none of the children that God has given to us shall be lost to the world; neither shall any become a child of perdition, in Jesus name. May God do mighty things in the lives of your children in response to your effectual and fervent prayers, in Jesus name, Amen!

OTHER BOOKS
BY PASTOR O.J KUYE

Discover the mystery of getting ahead in life. And conquer the major battle over the greatness of your destiny!

Fresh insights on the principles of maximum fruitfulness in:

- Marriage
- Career
- Business
- Relationship

Eye opening truths & ground breaking revelations on the:

- Greatest Race
- Greatest Scientist
- Great Preachers
- Great Industrialists
- Biggest Corporation
- 1st World Richest Billionaire of this generation.

REVELATIONS ON:
How some of the greatest inventors, artistes, athletes, business men and women, professionals, and founder of the world's largest church overcame their challenges to become outstanding heroes.

CONTAINING:

- Tried and tested principles of success
- Real life transforming stories of achievers in various fields
- Your failure is not final but pathway to success.

CONTAINING:

- Accident as a phenomenon of life
- The mystery of the garment
- Divine help is always available etc

This book is a manual to equip us with relevant knowledge to secure ultimate victory in the battles of life.

A Publication of
Philson Inc.

4437 Matthew Road,
Grand Prairie, TX 75052
Tel: (817) 939-1075
E-mail: ojkuye@aol.com

Contact Information

If you have been impacted by this book and will like to share your experience, comment or testimony; or if you want further resources or will like to request for prayers or contact the author, please use the information below:

Pastor OJ. Kuye

4437 Matthew Road,
Grand Prairie, TX 75052

www.amazon.com/author/ojkuye

+1972-602-8959 . ojkuye@aol.com